LOVE, POWER & MONEY

LOVE, POWER & MONEY

FAMILY BUSINESS BETWEEN GENERATIONS

DEAN FOWLER with
PEG MASTERSON EDQUIST

Brookfield, Wisconsin

Published by Glengrove Publishing
17280 W. North Avenue, Suite 205
Brookfield, WI 53045

Material quoted in Chapter 2 from *Getting To Yes 2/E* by Roger Fisher,
William Ury and Bruce Patton. Copyright © 1981, 1991 by Roger Fisher and
William Ury. Adapted and reprinted by permission of Houghton Mifflin
Company. All rights reserved.

Material quoted in Chapter 4 adapted and reprinted by permission of
Harvard Business School Press. From *Hidden Champions: Lessons from 500 of
the World's Best Unknown Companies* by Herman Simon, Boston, MA 1996;
pp. 275-276. Copyright © 1996 by the Harvard Business School Publishing
Corporation. All rights reserved.

Publisher's Cataloging-in-Publication Data
Fowler, Dean R., Ph.D.
     Love, power and money: family business between generations / Dean
R. Fowler, Ph.D. and Peg Masterson Edquist — Brookfield, WI : Glengrove
Publishing, 2002.

          p.   ;   cm.
     ISBN: 0-9716284-0-8

     1.Family-owned business enterprises—Succession. 2. Family-owned
business enterprises—Management. 3. Industrial management. I. Edquist,
Peg Masterson. II. Title. III. Family business between generations
HD62.25 .F69   2002   2002101279
658/.045   —dc21   CIP

06 05 04 03 02 ♠ 5 4 3 2 1

Project Coordination by Jenkins Group, Inc. ♠ www.bookpublishing.com
Cover design by Kathie Collins

Printed in the United States of America

This book is dedicated to my family:

. . .to my second mother, Barbara Glennie, who just celebrated her ninetieth birthday. She has encouraged me to dream and pursue my passions since I was a teenager.

. . .to my sons, Keith and Paul, who have taught me what it means to be a father and continually challenge me to practice what I preach.

. . .to my wife, Marj, my love since childhood, whose music is a gift for my soul.

CONTENTS

PREFACE

by Dean Fowler

Stories give our lives meaning. They place the events of our lives in a context that expresses the subtle richness of our experiences. All cultures have stories they tell to transmit the values and ethos of a people. Whether told around a campfire or around the kitchen table, our stories transmit what is important to those who speak and those who listen.

The stories of families in business are woven by intertwining the threads of love, power and money. Love binds together family life, empowering families to meet business challenges, but it can also entangle them in emotional turmoil. Power energizes decisive action necessary for the business marketplace, yet a struggle for control may tear a family apart. Money enhances the quest to meet goals, but it can trigger family disputes over fairness and equity.

This book tells the stories of numerous families in business collected over the past eighteen years in my consulting practice. But before telling their stories, let me share how I became passionately committed to the emotional health of such families.

My story begins in the fall of 1981, when I received a phone call from the pastor of my church. "Dean," he began, "as you may remember, a group of business executives from our church meets every other week for fellowship and Bible study. We've been talking a lot about ethics and business lately, and I think we need some help. Would you be willing to visit the group, give us some background on the ethical dilemmas facing executives and facilitate our discussions?"

So began my journey into the world of family business. At the time I was teaching undergraduate and graduate courses in theology as a full-time member of the faculty of Marquette University in Milwaukee, Wisconsin. I was fascinated by the challenges facing these executives, some of whom worked for Fortune 500 companies, but the majority of whom owned family businesses. Their issues were not academic. They were personal.

After my initial meetings as a guest speaker, I joined the group. In 1983, through their support and encouragement, I decided to leave the ivory towers of the university and joined a well-known consulting firm, The Executive Committee (TEC), that provided peer group facilitation and strategic planning services for the CEOs and presidents of businesses.

About 95 percent of my clients were the owners of family businesses. In fact, one of the peer groups I led was the continuation of the very first TEC group founded in 1954 for successors in family businesses. One of the original members of the group was still an active participant, but at age seventy he was now the chairman of the board of his family-owned business. Within a year, I had started a new group for young successors in family-owned businesses to complement my work with CEOs and presidents. In my role as group leader I met individually with each of my clients before every group meeting.

Recognizing my theological background and clinical training as a marriage and family therapist, my family business clients spoke with me not only about their business problems but also their personal stories. In each case, they shared stories involving the interplay among individual, family, business and ownership issues. For family business members, these issues were all part of one fabric, but most professionals specialized in just one area. These family business members were frustrated that no one was able to find integrated solutions to these complex issues. At the time, family business consulting had not yet emerged as a profession, and my clients said: "Dean, there is a real need for someone who can combine the personal dimension with family dynamics and the business issues. Why don't you specialize in family business consulting?"

So in 1988, Dean Fowler Associates, Inc. was born to deal with the emotional dynamics that have an impact on business strategy and succession planning.

The stories in *Love, Power and Money*, which draw on my experience with my family business clients, illustrate the common dynamics in family-owned companies. To protect the confidentiality of these families, the stories are composites of several families, with the names and details modified. While each story is unique, the basic themes are universal. The experiences of these families show the **critical importance of addressing the emotional dynamics of the family as the cornerstone for effective succession planning for the business**. Succession planning between generations is too often driven by the federal tax code, independent of the impact of such tax planning strategies on the life of the family—and often to the detriment of the business.

After an initial introduction to several families in Chapter 1, the second chapter explores the interplay between individuals and their family of origin, with an emphasis on the importance of effective communication. Families in business are somewhat unique in American culture because they are extended families of adults who have not just occasional but daily interaction with one another. Chapter 3 examines the interplay between the family and the business, with an emphasis on the guidelines for family employment. Chapter 4 addresses the business itself and the interplay between business strategy and the goals of the owners as individuals. The final two chapters focus attention on transitions facing families in business. Chapter 5 shows how the retirement of the senior generation must be coordinated with the emerging leadership of the next generation. Chapter 6 deals with the transfer of the ownership of the business to the successors.

In sharing their stories with you, I hope your family will learn from both the successes and failures of over 180 families in business who have been my clients during the past eighteen years. In each chapter we make suggestions concerning alternative approaches to resolving the common issues facing these business families. The selection of stories and the running commentary throughout the book have been designed to make the issues interesting and accessible to the general reader. I encourage your family members to read the book together and have the courage to discuss the themes that apply to your own situation.

To facilitate those discussions, you may want to use the questions at the end of each chapter as a guide. You may also want to use the assessments I have developed. The assessment process benchmarks your family against twelve critical success factors for families in business that parallel the topics covered in *Love, Power and Money*. The forty-five page Assessment Tool Report serves as a detailed discussion guide, with suggested action plans tailored to your family business. Family discussion might seem awkward at first, but if you start discussing the undiscussables in your family and your business, you will foster a much smoother passage between generations.

The Family Business Assessment Tool™

The importance of effective communication is one of the major themes of *Love, Power and Money*. Too many families in business have difficulty "discussing the undiscussables," and as a result let issues fester until they erupt into major conflicts that may jeopardize both the family and the business. I developed an assessment process to help families get these issues out on the table and to provide a structured format for resolving the issues most critical to any family business—whether those issues be between generations or among siblings and cousins who own a business together.

The process begins by having all of the stakeholders—parents, siblings, in-laws, non-family managers, and outside advisors—complete a questionnaire. The questions cover the broad range of topics facing closely held businesses and are similar to those at the end of each chapter of this book. The questionnaires may be completed on the Internet or filled out on a paper answer sheet and faxed back for scoring.

Once the questionnaires have been completed, we prepare a comprehensive report based on the diverse responses from all the participants. The report provides both graphic summaries and written interpretations covering twelve major factors facing the business. It identifies misconceptions and false expectations as well as positive foundations for the future of the family business. In addition, the report benchmarks your results against the scores of hundreds of respondents who have completed the assessment worldwide. The customized report provides an enlightened "emotional audit" of how family members perceive their relationships to the business.

The assessment process has been thoroughly researched at the University of Wisconsin-Milwaukee for reliability and validity. The research findings have shaped the topics covered in this book so that *Love, Power and Money* may be used as a study guide for families who have completed an assessment.

For more information about The Family Business Assessment Tool™ and to start the process with your family, please either visit our Web site www.deanfowler.com or call us at 800-203-3071.

THE AUTHORS

Dean R. Fowler, Ph.D. CMC

One of the world's leading family business experts, Dean R. Fowler received his Ph.D. in religion from Claremont Graduate University in Claremont, California, and is a Wisconsin state-certified marriage and family therapist. He is recognized by the Institute of Management Consultants as a Certified Management Consultant (CMC) and by the Family Firm Institute as a Family Business Advisor with Fellow Status.

After teaching in the graduate and undergraduate schools of Marquette University in Milwaukee, Wisconsin, he joined an international consulting firm committed to increasing the effectiveness and enhancing the lives of chief executive officers. Through the encouragement of his clients, he formed his own consulting firm to address the unique needs of families in business. In addition to Dean Fowler

Associates, Inc., he is a principal in Northern Oak Private Equity, a firm that designs plans to meet the capital and liquidity needs of closely held and family-owned businesses. He has served hundreds of families in business by resolving the emotional issues that have an impact on business strategy and succession planning. For more information, see www.deanfowler.com

Peg Masterson Edquist

Peg Masterson Edquist is a freelance journalist with more than twenty years of broadcast journalism and print journalism experience. During her career, she has worked for the *Milwaukee Journal/Sentinel, Inc.* as a business writer, covering beats as varied as retailing and the brewing industry.

During her freelance career, she has written for publications that include *Advertising Age*, the in-flight magazine for Midwest Express Airlines and *Photo District News*. She was a broadcast reporter for the *Business Journal of Greater Milwaukee* for thirteen years and also writes for the publication. Her husband, Jerry, is president of Carlson Tool & Manufacturing, Inc., a $16 million manufacturing firm with 115 employees. Carlson is a privately held, family-owned business founded by Jerry's father in 1958.

# ACKNOWLEDGMENTS

Without the families who have taught me about their successes and failures, this book would not have been possible. Each family is unique, and found its own solutions to the transitional issues facing their family business. But each family also shares in the common dynamics facing every family business—dynamics that have shaped the chapters of this book. Therefore, I thank the family businesses who have been my clients during the past eighteen years.

Several persons have been particularly influential in my career. In particular, I want to thank Bonnie and Bill Stafford, who provided encouragement and support during the time that I made the transition from Marquette University to The Executive Committee (TEC), an international consulting organization. At TEC both Jim Handy and Rex Coryell served as my mentors as I first worked with family business owners and provided facilitation of presidents' roundtables as well as a family business successors' group.

My deepest appreciation to Al Curtis, Duane Draheim, Rick Friedman, Bob Krahn, Ron Krizek, Mark Shiller and John Torinus, who read drafts of the chapters and suggested ways to improve the book. Also, my thanks to my executive assistant, Pam Shudy, who has spent numerous hours typing and retyping various versions of the manuscript.

Peg Masterson Edquist provided the warmth and human touch to the stories told in this book. She challenged me to make sure the book would be accessible to families in business, and shared her own passion for family enterprise throughout our collaboration.

Finally, I thank Marj, my wife, who has given me her love and support through the transitions in our family and in my career. She has proofread my newsletters for the past ten years and offered invaluable perspective to me in all of my endeavors. In particular, she has contributed to this book by reading early manuscripts, offering suggestions and, finally, proofreading the entire manuscript several times prior to publication.

Confidentiality Statement

Since 1983 I have been privileged to work with over 180 family-owned businesses. The owners and families of these businesses have taught me about the challenges they face, and have demonstrated both the measures of success and the root causes of failure facing their businesses as they have lived through the transition between generations.

Confidentiality is critically important to all families in business. Therefore, all of the stories used throughout this book are composite hypotheticals, drawing on specific situations I have encountered but never identifying the families involved. The stories illustrate the issues that face most family businesses in one way or another, but none of the stories represent a real situation. All have been disguised by combining common trends from several cases, inventing the names of family members and changing the names and locations of the businesses and other related characteristics. These changes have been made to make the real sources unrecognizable. Given these changes, any similarity to a real family business case is purely coincidental, unintended and unknown to me.

LOVE, POWER & MONEY

INTRODUCTION

by Peg Masterson Edquist

Not too long ago our business was in a cycle of back to back prosperous years. We were young, second-generation owners of a thriving manufacturing company and felt as if nothing could stand in our way of greatness. My husband's father, who had started the business, was now chairman of the board and maintained close contact with the company through weekly meetings. He was proud of the way things had progressed through the succession plan and the way my husband was performing in his role as president. At one point, when my husband was commiserating with his dad about what he felt was a banner year for the company, his wise father cautioned him, "Things won't always be this good." Initially deflated by the comments, my husband took them to heart and wondered if there could ever come such a time.

It did. We are currently experiencing one of our weakest periods in more than a decade, brought on by a collection of circumstances. Personnel problems, weak foreign markets, economic uncertainty and the changing global environment have created erratic sales trends and left us gasping for breath. Before the downturn we felt confident we could grow the company at a record pace, change the corporate culture to reflect a more evolved structure, institute infrastructure to accommodate the changes and aggressively pay off debt. In hindsight, our miscalculation about our ability to handle all of those things at once gave us false confidence. Remembering the wise comment by the elder generation left us feeling as if we had learned a hard lesson. But having that elder generation there for us was also a comfort at a time when loyalty and business can be mutually exclusive. It is the core of what a family business is all about.

Being involved in a family business has so many dimensions that it is almost impossible to explain the dynamics to an outsider. The ties that bind can be as loving and nurturing as an umbilical chord or as treacherous as a noose. Family relationships can be difficult enough; combining those relationships with a work environment can be nearly impossible. In helping to write this book, I learned about dozens of families and their working relationships with each other as members of a family business. Some families were inspiring; others left me shuddering that people could become so clouded in judgment. One of the clearest impressions I came away with was appreciating what a solid and loving family (business) I had married into. They had done things the right way, and as a result the company has entered the new millennium with confidence and staying power. My story, like others in this book, should inspire family business owners to avoid similar mistakes, learn from their own mistakes and take on issues before they become problems. I share this story here:

The day after my husband was born, more than four decades ago, his father entered the maternity ward and requested that his wife sign another mortgage on their home to start a tool and die plant in a converted garage. A solid marriage and seven children with this man gave my mother-in-law the confidence to sign the document, knowing that her husband would make good on his promise to always provide for her and the family. Several years and one more baby after it was founded, the company moved into a larger space, hired more employees and began a journey to join the thousands of small family-owned businesses in America. At that time, my husband was in third grade and not too concerned with anything beyond the next recess. It wasn't until he was nearly out of high school that he had thoughts of working in the family business. Instead of becoming a tool and die craftsman like his father, he became an engineer, working for the company during his summers home from college. Upon graduating, he decided he would try to work in the business full time in an engineering capacity. His father was just beginning to put into place a succession plan—a notion that many entrepreneurial founders frequently delay.

While there are seven other siblings in the family, only one other son was involved in the business at the board level. Although he no longer serves in that capacity, he is still my husband's greatest sounding board and would help with any business problem at a moment's notice. The family is immeasurably close, and has welcomed me as another addition to an already large clan. When I met my husband, he was still contemplating where his true career path lay. He loved the business, but he also wondered if he should explore other career options before making the decision to stay. I asked him where his true passion was, and he told me it was with the company. We married the next year, and in 1994 he became president, the day after our third child was born.

The company has grown along with our children, and we have only begun to experience the cycles of business life that lie ahead. As a business writer, I take great interest in all aspects of the company, and I dare say I am just as excited as my husband is over the prospects of growing a business. We, too, must look to succession in about a decade, and so the circle of family business life will continue.

Our story is like so many in this book, and yet all are different. They have drama, adventure and consequences. They are stories of families commingled with business triumphs and setbacks. Dean Fowler has facilitated hundreds of family business forums and consulted with many, many people who are at various stages of a family business cycle. He has seen what works and what can spell disaster. I hope each story intrigues and enlightens you and allows you to take away some insight that can make your family business more successful and strong for coming generations. From personal experience as well as the research done for this book, it's clear to me that making the right decisions at the right time is crucial for a family business to survive. Ignoring the tough decisions does not make them go away. Family ties are forever, as is the lasting legacy of a business run by the next generation. Perpetuating a dream can only be accomplished with your eyes wide open.

HAPPILY
EVER AFTER

Chapter 1

Love, power and money are three critical forces shaping the essence of family business dynamics today. Finding balance among the three is the key to family business continuity, yet very few family businesses successfully transfer the ownership and management of their corporation to the next generation. The fact is, 86.7 percent of family business owners who have chosen a successor select one of their children to carry on the family tradition,[1] but only 30 percent of family businesses are actually able to keep the business in the family.[2] The parent's success becomes the child's failure—an allegorical tale retold throughout the world.

---

1 Arthur Anderson/MassMutual, *American Family Business Survey* (Springfield, MA: MassMutual, 1997), 12.
2 John L. Ward, *Keeping the Family Business Healthy: How to Plan for Continuing Growth, Profitability and Family Leadership* (San Francisco: Jossey-Bass Management Series, 1987), 1-2, 247-250.

A fundamental reason for this failure is that too many families design their estate transfer plans to meet the requirements of the federal tax code—requirements dealing with money, not love or power. A noble thought, but money alone fails to address the underlying forces shaping the family and the business. The fact that millions of dollars are saved in taxes does not compensate for a family torn apart by divergent needs, or a business out of control with no leadership. So while the tax code provides parameters that can be used to transfer wealth, the future success of a family business rests somewhere else, a somewhere else that remains uncharted waters for most business owners.

But it is in navigating these waters that the success or failure of the business and often the family is crafted. Who will run the business? Are equity and fairness synonymous? How will the ownership control of the business protect its ability to compete? How will decisions be made? How will the corporation position itself strategically in a constantly changing marketplace? Too often crises drive family business transitions as families react to conflicts rather than design plans where love, power and money converge to create a smooth transition between the generations. Here are some common scenarios:

- The gifting of minority shares of stock to multiple successors creates a crisis in leadership by initiating a struggle for power.
- Misplaced priorities regarding tax-saving strategies cause poor decisions in the distribution of assets among the inheritors. In turn, parents' loving concern for the fair treatment of their children is undermined.
- Sibling rivalry emerges over issues of business control.
- Inactive shareholders desire financial rewards for ownership that run counter to the needs of the business.
- Conflicts emerge about how business proceeds are distributed among the competing interests of the business, the active managers and the inactive owners.

After the death of a founder or majority shareholder, a crisis in leadership often undermines both the family and the business.

Losing a parent is difficult enough; losing the captain of the ship can spell disaster. In preparing for critical times of transition, goals for both the business and the family must be clarified. While most families minimize their federal tax exposure through good legal advice, too few design a plan for the future of the business that is integrated with the changing needs of the family. For example, some successors may want to leave the business at a future date to pursue their own interests, so they need a plan to sell their stock in the corporation. Will the desire to sell stock at a fair market value be consistent with the tax planning strategies developed for the ownership transition of the business?

TOO MANY COOKS SPOIL THE BUSINESS

Almost every business owner is concerned with the prospect that the government will someday get too much of the business that has been a life's work. That concern is accompanied by the desire to provide for the financial security of the surviving spouse for the remainder of his or her lifetime. Invariably, business owners want to explore every opportunity that maximizes the amount of equity that remains in the hands of the family. But in their attempts to save taxes and protect their spouses, owners often face unpleasant decisions about the fair distribution of their assets and often fail to address issues concerning the control of the company.

In part, the dilemma of power is rooted in the tax code itself. For family business transfers, the federal tax code favors splitting the ownership of a company into the hands of a new group of owners, each with a minority interest in the firm. The dollar value of stock owned by a minority shareholder for tax purposes might be as much as 40 percent less than stock owned by a majority shareholder who thereby controls the corporation. Why? Because discounts are recognized for the lack of control and limited marketability of the stock. With restricted minority shares, hefty discounts from the full market value may be taken on the value of the stock for gifting and estate transfer purposes, keeping transfer taxes as low as possible—a positive feature when stock is gifted. In addition, most parents want to treat their children equally. Since the company usually represents their major asset, parents elect to gift shares in equal proportion to each of their children. Consequently, most estate plans for family business owners involve the gifting of restricted, minority shares of stock in the corporation to the children of the owners. But in most plans, the future governance and voting control of the corporation remain unresolved. Equal ownership may mean that everyone, in the long run, gets an equal vote, but it puts no one at the helm. For businesses where the control of the corporation was previously in the hands of one strong-willed owner, the new company may be like a play without a director—loud, noisy and without purpose.

Most owners hope that the successor children will work closely together and make decisions that protect both the business and the family. However, hope and reality are often incompatible. Let's see how four families dealt with their hopes and realities during the ownership transitions facing their family businesses.

The Brown Family
The dynamics of power

On a hot August afternoon in 1978, Ted Brown stepped from his attorney's office, satisfied that the papers he'd just signed would provide financial security for his wife and family in the future. As he watched thunderclouds build on the horizon of the farming community he knew so well, Ted Brown had no way to know that he'd just created a different kind of storm that would someday embroil his wife and children in conflicts over the control of the business.

Ted Brown quit farming after World War II and started an agricultural equipment parts distribution business. Ted was a natural. Born and raised on the family farm, he knew what farmers needed, what the market would need and how to put it all together. The result was an extremely successful business that grew up around Ted's birthplace. Ted lived in the country with his family and started the business by serving the farmers in his own community. The business quickly blossomed into a parts supply company and expanded into the barn. As the business grew, warehouse buildings and truck distribution facilities sprouted up around the farmhouse. They exist in that configuration today: the old family farmhouse surrounded by a bustling distribution company.

Ted and his wife, Helen, had four children; one daughter and three sons. Two sons worked in the business—one managed the warehouse operations while the other oversaw the trucking fleet. Fifteen years ago Ted Brown died, leaving the two sons active in the business in charge of the day-to-day management of the company. On that August day in 1978, Ted had completed the recapitalization of the corporation into two classes of stock, voting and nonvoting. Over the years before his death, about 90 percent of the nonvoting stock had been gifted to his children. However, he and his wife retained 100 percent of the voting control of the corporation, and at his death this voting control was held entirely by his wife. According to their plan, her voting shares would be divided equally among the four children at the time of her death. During Helen's lifetime, however, she had ultimate control of major business decisions. She valued family harmony and desired that her children get along with one another without conflict.

Every morning, her two sons active in the business, as well as two long-time, nonfamily employees (who had been Ted Brown's trusted managers) would hold their operations meeting in Helen's farmhouse kitchen, sipping coffee Helen made for the group every day. Helen had a known heart condition, and her health was fragile at best. With any disagreement or conflict at the meeting, Helen's heart would race and her blood pressure would soar. Not surprisingly, the family and managers sidestepped any conflict and did not discuss major differences in front of Helen. So while Helen's fragile health put a lid on visible conflict, the underlying tensions did not go away. Decisions were made, but by exception. And while the family appeared to be doing well on the surface, conflict over key business issues remained, like a wicked undertow beneath a calm ocean.

When Helen died several years ago, her voting shares were divided equally among her four children, leaving no one person with control over corporate decisions. The plan Ted had signed on that hot August afternoon in 1978 had become a blueprint for strife. Because family members had avoided conflict during their mother's lifetime, the potential for conflict to get out of control under the new system was high, and it erupted within three days of Helen's death.

The oldest brother, John, who was in charge of the warehouse operations, felt that without his contributions, the business would fail. He demanded that he be named president and, furthermore, demanded that his three siblings each sign a legal agreement transferring their voting shares of the company over to his control. The previously contained conflict between Helen's children suddenly erupted. His sister agreed to support John, but his two brothers vowed to fight his grab for power. They were split in a fifty-fifty battle over control. While his brothers respected his business ability, they did not trust him with total control of the whole business, their primary asset.

Working with the corporate attorney, John told his brothers that if they did not agree to his request for control, he would exercise his option under the buy-sell agreement to sell his stock back to the corporation based on an objective valuation of the company. Power and money stood center stage in the family conflict.

John's demands created a serious conflict within the family, not only over the control of the business, but also because the tax liabilities from Helen's estate had not been determined. Certainly for estate planning purposes, the stock needed to be valued as low as possible to minimize taxes. But from John's perspective, the stock needed to be valued as high as possible so he could cash out if not empowered as president. Attorneys for the siblings urged them to find a workable solution with John so that he would not bring the battle to court, which could potentially drive up the value of the stock, creating a tax burden for the whole family.

POWER CANNOT EXIST IN A VACUUM

The Brown family case study illustrates how the battle for power within a corporation is often precipitated by the death of the second primary shareholder—in this case, the death of Helen Brown. The family estate plan needed more than an equal division of property and buy-sell agreements. It needed a structure to give the group of minority owners a method for making critical decisions regarding the management of the business.

To resolve these issues of control and the conflict precipitated by John's demands for power, the Brown siblings developed a new method of governing the company, through a legally empowered board of directors. Since there were an even number of shareholders (the four Brown children), three nonfamily board members were elected to the board with full voting power. This gave the family the power to make all decisions when they agreed on critical issues, but provided a mechanism to end deadlock among the shareholders if they were split fifty-fifty over policies or corporate strategy.

The board had four primary roles: First, it had the power to elect a president for the corporation, either a family member or a non-family executive with expertise necessary to lead the company. Second, it had the power to approve the operating budget of the company that had been developed by the management team. Third, it determined whether major capital expenditures needed to be made to support growth requirements. Finally, the board had the power to approve the strategic plan for the company that had been developed formally by the key managers of the company. The strategic plan defined the primary operating responsibilities and accountability criteria for all the managers, including employed family members. In other words, the shareholders could protect their financial investment as owners but could not control the day-to-day decisions of management. The president, elected by the board, had primary day-to-day responsibility but was accountable to the board.

The development of a formal board and the distinction between management roles and ownership rights provided a new, positive context for the Brown family members to manage the business. Although John was elected president, he did not have ultimate power and authority. He was held accountable to the board, and could lose his position if he did not meet the expectations of the board, based on pre-established company performance standards. The process worked so well that the business has continued to grow successfully. Through the board of directors, the family ownership group has a structure for dealing with their differences while at the same time sharing involvement in determining the future of the business.

As an alternative to a formal board of directors, some family businesses legally empower a third person to break deadlocks between shareholders. This is the approach Joyce Thomas took when she realized that she was being forced to choose between her sons.

The Thomas Family
The pressures of love

Bill Thomas founded and owned a company that manufactured metal stamping components for the automotive industry. Bill and his wife, Joyce, had two sons, Sean and Joseph, who worked in the business. According to their estate plan, Joyce inherited 60 percent of the voting stock of the company upon Bill's death. The estate plan, in giving Joyce voting control, did what it was intended to do—protect her financial future. The remaining 40 percent of the voting stock was divided equally between Sean and Joseph.

Joyce Thomas had never been active in the business and had little knowledge of, or interest in, the management and strategic issues facing the company. For a time after Bill's death, the business continued to be profitable. No major changes were required in corporate strategy and everyone was happy with the progress the business made. Several years later, however, the marketplace changed dramatically. The auto industry was moving into plastic parts and other types of composite materials in vehicles. Manufacturers of metal stampings faced declining sales. Companies were either growing in new ways or falling behind the competition. During this period the company posted a loss for the first time in its history. The market was shrinking and the company needed to think about a strategic change in order to survive. While the Brown family had faced a major conflict at the time of the death of their mother, the Thomas family faced a major conflict when the business faltered due to changing market conditions during their mother's lifetime.

Sean and Joseph had different strategies for handling the problem. Sean, who was president, was fairly aggressive, proposing a high-risk strategy that involved diversifying into new markets to make the company less dependent on its old products. His plan would require the acquisition of new machinery and equipment. Joseph, who was a vice president, wanted to take a more conservative approach. He wanted to cut prices and try to grow market share as much as possible as competitors failed. So long as the company enjoyed financial stability, Joyce operated well as the chief executive officer of the corporation. However, as the conflict between her sons intensified over the best strategy for the business, she found she was being thrust into the role of the "chief emotional officer." In this role, she struggled with how best to demonstrate her love for each of her children.

In spite of the fact that Sean was president, his title meant nothing when it came to control over business strategy. His mother had the voting control, and both brothers had the ear of their mother, arguing their own positions and hoping to influence her decisions. This left it up to Joyce to make the decision as to which strategy to follow. Joyce recalled too many evenings alone in her kitchen, sipping herbal tea and trying to find a solution. "There was enormous agony and tears for me," she said. "How can you choose one son over another?"

As the brothers became deadlocked over several critical decisions involving the company, Joyce recognized the need for a trusted person who could work as the "swing vote," essentially breaking stalemates between her sons. Without this swing vote, the two brothers could be deadlocked in every major decision. She feared that the tension between her sons would only intensify after her death. Joyce Thomas felt trapped. She realized that she did not have the business experience to make many of the critical choices facing the company and she felt any decisions she made would essentially force her to choose between her two sons.

A trusted friend of her late husband suggested she had three options: Either hire a nonfamily president to run the company, sell the business or empower a third party to take over the decision-making role when Sean and Joseph could not reach an agreement. Joyce wasn't enthusiastic about bringing in an outsider as president, no matter how experienced a businessperson he or she might be. She also refused to sell the business, since the business was a symbol of Bill's living legacy. Therefore, she took the third option, and empowered Bill's trusted friend to break deadlocks between her sons. To reinforce this decision, she re-wrote her own estate plan to transfer only 29 percent of her voting shares to each of her sons upon her death, so that neither alone would have control over the business. She placed the remaining 2 percent in a trust and empowered the trustee to break the deadlocks between her sons if necessary. So long as Sean and Joseph agreed with one another, they could operate the business without interference from the outside, but if they disagreed, a deadlock provision was now in place. In this way, Joyce was free to focus her attention on nurturing family relationships and loving her children. "It worked out well," Joyce said. "Now I do what I do best."

TRIMMING THE FAMILY TREE

When a family business undergoes transformation brought on by strategic business forces or when it faces financial turmoil driven by economic downturns, conflict between siblings actively employed in the business and those who are not employed, often intensifies. Business decisions made by the siblings active in the business become issues concerning the family's emotional legacy as well as the family's wealth. For many inactive family members, ownership of stock is symbolic of their emotional relationship with their parents. The stock has value as a legacy to be preserved and protected. The inactive siblings' desire to preserve this family legacy often comes in conflict with the active siblings' desire to keep the company current and competitive. Beyond the emotional component, strategic and economic forces often require tremendous financial investments that limit the ability of the business to pay any dividends or other financial rewards to the shareholders.

While the Brown and Thomas family cases have dealt with the tensions that emerge among those family members actively involved in the management of the business, the Titans had to face conflict between family on the outside and family on the inside.

The Titan Family
A legacy of money

The Titan Corporation is an established, $250-million manufacturing company founded by two brothers more than one hundred years ago. In 1910, the brothers became locked in a fierce struggle for control of the business. The differences between the brothers could not be resolved and the business split. One branch of the family formed a competing company and located it in the same town as the Titan Corporation.

The enterprise that bore the Titan name was successfully transferred to the next generation and was operated for many years by two of the founder's sons, Elmer and Lawrence, who planned to transfer the company to their respective sons, David and Jerry. While Elmer and Lawrence had lived and worked well together most of their lives, their own sons, David and Jerry, did not get along at all.

Over the years, the rivalry increased among the third-generation cousins. Because of past legacies of conflict among shareholders, the company had a "Solomon's Agreement" in place in case of deadlock.

According to this agreement, if there was unresolvable conflict among the owners, one family group could state a price for purchasing the stock of the other family, who in turn, had the option to either buy or sell at that price. Because of the ongoing tensions between David and Jerry, this agreement was exercised by David's side of the family, who then bought out the other family members. The family tree was trimmed and the Titan Corporation was once again owned by one family, but not without significant fallout. Despite their years of working together, the buyout bitterly divided Elmer and Lawrence, who broke all contact with each other.

While ownership and control of the business was resolved, at least temporarily, David recognized that conflict could arise again. Based on the family's history, David did not want the same controversy to tear apart his family and he wanted to avoid the problems that had plagued the Titans for two generations. "I didn't want my children to end up not speaking to each other someday," David acknowledged.

David's family, who now owns the Titan Corporation, includes his three children: Carl, president of the business; John, a professional working outside of the business; and Sarah, a homemaker who lives in a nearby community. Although Sarah has no active interest in the company, she sees the business as an emotional link to her past. She has a strong connection to her parents as well as to the company. Sarah has three children of her own under age fourteen, and she feels that her children should have a right to work in the family business and become managers when they are old enough and experienced enough to contribute to its success. Carl, the president, has two children, both under age fifteen.

From a family inheritance perspective, David made sure the minority shares of stock in the company had been transferred equally to all three of his children. However, because David knew that tensions could grow between Carl (who was employed in the business as its president) and his two children who were not employed, he created a trust to hold the voting shares of the business, and he named Carl as the trustee. Through this arrangement, Carl had control of the business. The trustee, however, could be replaced if certain business conditions were not met. According to the trust, if the president has not managed the business effectively and the company experiences a downturn in profits in any two consecutive years, the president (in this case Carl) loses his or her right to serve as the trustee of the voting trust. The owners can elect a new trustee, who then can hire a new president for the company.

Although David recognized that someone had to be in control, he had not anticipated the emotional response of his daughter when Carl decided to make some strategic changes in the way the business was positioned in the marketplace. Since Carl had to maintain profitability, he decided that he needed to drop one of the product lines that had been central to the business in the past. This line no longer carried high margins, and after an examination of alternatives, he determined that the line actually was a drain on business profitability. Carl's father, however, had founded this product line, and for a twenty-year period it defined much of the business. From Sarah's perspective, dropping the product line was tantamount to denying the company history. If the product line were dropped, Sarah felt an emotional legacy would be gone as well, a legacy that had became part of her self-image.

Relationships between Carl, John and Sarah had been peaceful for several years. When Carl proposed the change in strategy, he created a major disruption in the family. And while, as the trustee of the voting trust, he had the authority to make the decision, Carl did not anticipate the furor it would cause. "I was stunned by the emotion my sister, Sarah, attached to this change," Carl said at the time. "I thought it was the best thing for the business and I felt I had the evidence to prove it."

CARRYING EMOTIONAL BAGGAGE

How could Carl make Sarah feel that the family legacy would be preserved, and at the same time be able to make the strategic decisions necessary for the company's future?

To preserve harmony within the family, there had to be a way for Carl to make business decisions but also for Sarah to have a meaningful and significant way to honor the history of the family. To accomplish these alternatives, the family agreed to create a foundation that managed the significant charitable contributions of the company. Sarah chaired the foundation's board and met her needs to honor the family's past. In turn, Carl was able to make the necessary changes in the business, while his sister protected the family heritage.

"The only reason we were able to work it out," said Carl, "was because Sarah and I have a good relationship and we were able to talk about the underlying issues. We were able to see each other's side of the issues and to work things out. There was also a family history of conflict neither of us wanted to repeat."

Similar to the Titans, the Mathisons also needed to find a solution to the tensions that develop between shareholders who are employed in the business and those who are not. While the Titans resolved the tensions through the creation of a voting trust, the Mathisons decided it was best to sell the business to the son who was willing to make his life commitment to the success of the business. The Mathisons managed to effectively transfer the business from generation to generation without the company losing its entrepreneurial spirit.

The Mathison Family
Breaking eggs to make an omelet

John Mathison owned a manufacturing company that had developed a specialized, highly engineered mechanical device used throughout the machine tool industry. John patented his invention and developed a successful niche market for himself and his company, which generated revenues of just under $100 million a year. His business prospered and his family enjoyed the success that accompanies business growth.

His son, Todd, began to work in the company as soon as he completed college. A creative and talented engineer in his own right, Todd specialized in electronics and computer design rather than mechanical engineering, as his father had done. Although John's daughter, Sandy, and his wife, Kate, were not involved with the business, John wanted his wife, son and daughter to share equally in the assets of his estate. Yet, because he early on recognized and respected Todd's talents and interest in the company, John had already talked to Todd in depth about a plan that would transfer operating control of the company to him. Over dinner on a business trip, the father and son recognized and felt the respect and trust each had for the other. Todd pledged that if he were chosen to run the company, his mother and sister would share fully in the financial rewards. Little did Todd realize on the night he made his pledge to his father how quickly he would be tested. Three days after their trip, John Mathison died of a massive coronary, and Todd Mathison's life was changed forever.

Unfortunately, John Mathison had delayed the preparation of a new estate plan. When John died, the old plan went into effect, splitting ownership of the business three ways: To his son, to his daughter and to his wife. Although Todd and his father had agreed in principle on a plan regarding the stock and the eventual transfer of total ownership and control of the company to Todd, their plan was never legally implemented.

With the untimely death of her husband, Kate Mathison became emotionally attached to the company in a way that she had never been before. Although she had not been directly involved with the business before her husband's death, she now took an office at the company and came to work every day. Unlike her mother, Sandy remained uninvolved in the business.

Given the situation created by the estate plan, Todd felt an enormous obligation to his mother and sister. Since he owned only one-third of the company, Todd did not feel free to take financial risks that might jeopardize his mother's and sister's investment. While he had the entrepreneurial drive and vision that was characteristic of his father, he had the obligations of a professional manager—a hired gun. Todd knew that without significant reinvestment, the business would languish, so he proposed an arrangement that over time would allow him to buy out the interests of his mother and sister, assuming they were willing.

Todd was a talented electronics engineer who saw ways to expand the company's business, building on the accomplishments of his father. However, Todd did not really enjoy running the operations side of the business. Todd's entrepreneurial nature kept him focused on new business. Recognizing that he lacked the real desire to run business operations, Todd wisely chose to bring in an outsider. He hired a search firm to find a qualified company president to run the day-to-day functions, and recruiters found a respected executive from within the industry. Todd hired this executive, who became president, while Todd became chief executive officer. "I felt like I was putting an enormous puzzle together," Todd said. "With someone to run the existing business, I could go on to the next piece."

The next piece was developing new markets. Todd saw how electronics could breathe new life into the company's products and better serve the customer base that had supported the company for so many years. Under the new management, several employees were terminated, new ones were hired and the company changed its focus from simply mechanical equipment to computer-related products. Using his father's company as a base, Todd grew the new market segments successfully, and used the profits from these new business ventures to buy out his mother and sister.

Kate Mathison used the money from the purchase of her stock to set up a foundation that supported the engineering department of the local university, which her husband had attended. While he was alive, John Mathison had continued to be involved in the educational support of new engineers, and Kate wanted to honor his accomplishments through a foundation and an endowed chair in his name at the university. This gave her comfort as well as a lasting legacy to pass on to future generations of engineering graduates.

This effective arrangement enabled Todd to fulfill his obligations to his mother and sister while at the same time engaging his own entrepreneurial spirit.

A POUND OF PREVENTION

Each of the families discussed in this chapter faced tremendous estate planning challenges. Their plans were driven primarily by estate tax issues—the transfer of money rather than the dynamics of love and power. In each case, the families had to determine a new structure for the leadership of the corporation, one that had not been defined by the estate plan. The Brown siblings became deadlocked over power issues shortly after the death of their mother. The Thomas family needed a method for setting new strategic directions in their business during a time that the matriarch was still living; however, the company was paralyzed at first because she did not know how to choose between the competing strategies proposed by her sons. The Titans had to resolve the emotional challenges that developed when the legacy of the business was threatened by new demands of the marketplace. The Mathisons had to balance the entrepreneurial drive of the son active in the business with the financial security needs of the rest of the family.

Each of the families discovered its own solution. The Browns established a board of directors. The Thomases named a deadlock trustee. The Titans created a voting trust. The Mathisons structured a buyout of the inactive shareholders. Each approach provided a new governance structure that met the unique needs of the family and the business.

Unfortunately, each of these four families found solutions only after struggling through serious conflicts. Business success and family harmony are more effectively addressed when the family develops an estate plan that grows out of the broader needs of all family members. Success comes when the plan is built on the foundation of good communication, shared values, an appreciation of the needs of the business and a vision for both the family and the company. Successful transition plans between the generations take into account both the changing needs of the business and the diverse interests, perspectives and needs of the family members—they find a balance between the emotional needs of the family (love), the leadership needs of the business (power) and the financial needs of the owners (money).

The interplay of love, power and money shapes the remaining chapters of this book. Ultimately the effective convergence of the three is grounded in discussing the undiscussables—in being open as a family to talk about different needs. A strong family network is the unshakable base upon which a successful family business stands, and this cannot exist without effective communication.

Questions to Discuss About Your Family Business:

Although it may be difficult to get started at first, especially if your family has not had these kinds of discussions, it is important to the long-term health of your company to discuss what are often undiscussables. If conflict runs high in your family, consider using an experienced facilitator to help guide your family conversations on these topics:

+ What issues facing your family business might erupt into major conflicts in the future?

+ What are the undiscussables in your family business that need to be discussed and then resolved?

+ If your family encounters conflicts over power and money, what vehicles do you have in place to foster effective communication?

+ Did you identify with any of the families in this chapter? What elements of their situation are similar to your own? Would the solutions they found work for your family business? Which ones?

THE TIES THAT BIND

Chapter 2

W hy are some families in business so successful in balancing the needs of the family with the success of their businesses, while other families are plagued by conflict, disruption and dysfunction? Experiences of family-owned businesses show that there is a necessary transition from a family of children to a family of adults that makes continued success possible. This foundation—the transition to adulthood—lays the groundwork for dealing with other issues the business faces, particularly succession in management and the transfer of ownership to future generations.

Many families focus their energy on the technical aspects of transitions, such as effective estate planning and the development of the organization, its structure and its management needs. While these are important issues, not enough families pay attention to the more fundamental questions of whether the next generation has achieved maturity and, most importantly, strong self-esteem. Without this healthy personal development, few individuals will be successful both as adults in the family and as contributors to the business.

While the primary goal of a family with young children is to provide an environment that fosters emotional growth so the children develop into self-sufficient adults, the goals of an *adult* family, which includes the *adult* successor generation, are somewhat different. The adult family must encourage the individual development and self-direction of all the members. This allows the young adults to enter into their own independent world, built on a strong sense of self-worth and self-esteem.

The roots that nourish adult development grow during childhood. Consequently, long-range success for family-owned businesses is grounded in the early life of the family, during which the children learn about values, resolving conflicts, communicating effectively and, most importantly, finding their own sense of worth.

To build strong self-esteem, young adults need to feel accepted and appreciated by their parents. But for many families with a business, it is the business that becomes the primary focus—the other "child" in the family. Family members may frequently feel torn between their sense of duty to the business and the desire to pursue their own interests that have no connection to the business. They hope that by staying with the company, they will find a way to achieve recognition and "approval" from family members and to avoid being disconnected and cut off from the family. Underlying this is the knowledge that it is the business that has provided for them all these growing-up years, and the business, like pagan gods of old, demands its sacrifices.

Often the children of family business owners move directly from the home or school to the business. Consequently, many young adults involved in a family enterprise don't deal with normal adult transition issues until after they have been employed at the business for ten to fifteen years. They find that establishing themselves as separate adults is difficult, because working with family members maintains the dynamics and patterns characteristic of childhood. In families where the founder is domineering and controlling, it is even harder for the children to learn self-sufficiency.

Yet by their mid-thirties, successors have established themselves in the business and typically begin to want to be separate and independent. But existing family structure has locked them into roles that leave them frustrated and unable to assert their autonomy. The bonds of family culture and history turn out to be the strongest of all.

The road to a successful future is possible in family businesses where parents and children are able to redefine their relationships on an adult basis. To reach the adult position, children must shift from dependence on their parents to independence, creating a foundation for their own choices and decisions. This transition to adulthood is important for successors in family businesses as they decide either to enter the business or choose alternative careers. Many family business experts recommend that young adults find employment outside the business before committing to the company. There are two advantages gained by this decision: First, the obvious business experience accumulated and second, the emotional independence achieved. The emotional separation is critical for building personal authority, self-esteem and self-confidence. The establishment of the young adult's personal authority becomes the foundation for redefining the historical communication patterns between parents and their children.

This chapter explores four different family business situations in which the dynamics of this child-to-adult development shaped the problems facing the family and the business.

The Greylock Family
Breaking from tradition

Peter Greylock started his business as a craftsman during World War II. His small metalworking shop gradually expanded to include other small metal fabrication operations and eventually grew to become a rather successful business. Peter's oldest son, Scott, joined the business after earning a degree in business administration. His younger son, Tim, decided to pursue a career outside of the family business and showed no interest in ever working at the company. After Scott had been employed for fifteen years, Peter, then sixty-two years old, started to think about retirement. Then one October afternoon, after a Saturday round of golf, Peter had a stroke and was hospitalized. The event precipitated an emotional struggle between the father and son that lasted more than two years.

The medical emergency focused Peter's attention on the need for estate planning, since to date he had only drafted a simple will. In order to treat both of his children equally, he drew up an inheritance agreement that distributed half of the assets of the business to Scott, who was working at the company. The other half went to Tim, who lived in Florida and was not involved in the business.

Peter Greylock decided he wanted to retire when he left the hospital, but after his lengthy recuperation, which lasted more than ten months, he opted to delay his retirement. This put Scott, now in his early forties and actively involved in the day-to-day management of the business, in an awkward position. He had successfully run the business during his father's illness, and now the elder Greylock was back and excited to be involved once again in making the day-to-day decisions that Scott had been making.

Peter, on the other hand, felt that while his son was a capable administrator and had done a good job of learning the business, he lacked leadership skills and dealt poorly with conflict. Although he continued to give Scott more management control, Peter's presence at the company caused Scott to feel he was being constantly second-guessed.

Scott continued to feel increasingly frustrated and depressed. His tendency to avoid conflict prevented him from discussing his father's leaving the business. This went on for several years, which adversely affected the business, leaving sales flat at best. Neither Peter nor Scott Greylock truly wanted to share the spotlight, both wanting to be in control of the business. They needed an intermediary to help them negotiate an approach that better met each one's personal needs.

Peter Greylock recognized there was a problem, and at Tim's urging they hired me as their family business consultant. Since Peter questioned Scott's leadership abilities, I recommended that a "mentor" be hired to help Scott develop good business leadership skills. I felt that Scott needed to find confidence from some source other than his father. Scott needed someone with whom he could discuss business issues and alternatives as well as receive advice when tough decisions had to be made. I knew several extremely competent business executives who had recently retired from the presidencies of their respective companies. Scott and his father interviewed these executives, then selected one to work on a part-time basis as Scott's mentor. Working with the mentor, Scott began to make dramatic changes to improve the business. Unlike Scott, the mentor was much more decisive and willing to deal with confrontation. He recommended that Peter retire and stay out of the day-to-day decision making, while Scott worked with the mentor on a plan to improve the business' profitability. Peter could approve the plans at the board level.

With his mentor's guidance and support, Scott terminated two people he'd vacillated about removing for some time. He brought in a new accountant and a new administrative manager the first year and then a new plant manager the second year. As is often the case with strongly entrepreneurial companies, the key managers who were fired had worked with Peter and had been used to simply carrying out his orders. They were the privates and Peter was the general. Scott's style of management was one of a team. He needed contributors—people willing to share in the demands of management.

In time, Scott built a management team with business expertise and the ability to share responsibilities as a group. Six months into the second year, profits doubled, and in the next two years the company experienced its highest sales and earnings in its history. In reality, Scott proved to be a good leader, but not the type of leader that his father had been, and not a leader of the same people who were loyal to his father. Scott needed his own team, one that would work effectively under his style of leadership. The mentor saw this difference in style and took action to help Scott restructure his father's business. The mentor's strategy was to help Scott build a management team that shored up Scott's weaker areas by bringing in qualified individuals. Scott realized that with this new organization, both he and the business could be successful. And he discovered that the business could be profitable—in fact, more profitable than it had been under his father's leadership—through the enlistment of capable managers. Today, Scott, who recently turned fifty, wants to retire in five years and sell his stake in the company to the management team.

During this transition, it was clear that the emotional dynamics of the family relationship took the focus away from the business. When the relationship shifted from Scott and his father to Scott and the mentor, Scott accepted his limitations and realized it was appropriate to hire new managers from outside the business to play a key role in running the company, an alternative his father had never accepted. A common tension between senior and successor generations occurs when an entrepreneurial parent measures the children by the old, familiar standards, rather than by the new needs of a growing and changing company. Despite the fact that at first Scott hadn't met his father's expectations, Scott proved he could play an important—although different—role in the business. With the company now profitable and Peter Greylock fully retired, Scott was able to demonstrate his managerial effectiveness by working with an excellent team of senior executives, a team that someday would buy the business from the family.

SAVING FACE WHILE SHARING THE SPOTLIGHT

As the Greylock story shows, the needs and desires of parents and their children often conflict over the leadership of the family business. On the one hand, as an entrepreneur, Peter's self-esteem and meaning in life were bound up with the business. He felt most alive when at work and, therefore, after recovering from his stroke wanted to be re-invigorated by business activities. On the other hand, Scott needed space to be his own man and not operate under the shadow of his father. The outside mentor provided an excellent buffer between Peter and his son, so that conflicts over business leadership did not undermine their ability to be father and son to one another.

Such tensions between parents and their children are often manifested when the successors take on leadership roles in the family business. To avoid these conflicts, many successors decide to pursue their own interests rather than carry the mantle of the legacy of the family business.

The Buttner Family
Loving the family but not the business

Paul Buttner, age fifty, is president and CEO of Buttner Clothing Manufacturers, Inc., makers of upscale hunting clothing and equipment. His father, now seventy-three, founded the business forty years ago and is currently retired. Paul Buttner has two children: Pamela, twenty-seven and George, twenty-four. Like many second-generation owners, he wants to keep the business in the family. Pamela announced at an early age that she had no interest in pursuing the family business and currently works as a writer for a major magazine in New York City. Driven by his need to have the family business continue into the third generation, Paul Buttner realized that he would need to groom his son as his successor if the business were to continue as a family enterprise.

With his father's encouragement and support, George attended college to study retail merchandising. Although lacking in experience, George landed a job at a large retail store in Chicago, due in part to his father's contacts. George's retail experience in Chicago was meant to provide a useful background for George before he entered the family business.

George had been fairly close to his father throughout his adolescence, sharing similar personalities and hunting together every fall. Although George felt no direct pressure to succeed his father in the business, he did feel the need to please his father and felt the retail business was something he was willing to explore. He reasoned that several years of experience away from the family company would give him a valuable outside perspective. It did, but not in the way that his father had hoped.

While working in Chicago, George struggled with his job. He came to dislike the retail field, where he felt the relationships and rewards were shallow and without meaning. In addition, George did not share his father's affinity for business. When getting up and going to work each day left his stomach in knots, George knew it was time to re-examine his direction. The only positive experience was the discovery that he truly enjoyed teaching the people who'd been assigned to work with him in the company training program. The sharing of experience and knowledge, even in the retail business, gave him a sense of personal satisfaction. He volunteered as an English tutor at a neighborhood school and loved every minute. George had found his path, but it would not be an easy one.

George talked to friends and to his older sister. When he returned home, after living and working in Chicago for two years, George explained to his mother that he did not want to stay in the retail business and did not plan to go into the family business. Instead, he told her he had decided to register immediately for classes in teacher education. Intuitively, George knew how hurt his father would be. Unable to face his father directly about his choice and fearing his father's keen disappointment, George left him a letter explaining his decision and apologizing. As might have been expected, Paul Buttner was devastated to learn of his son's decision indirectly, and for some time could not speak to George. He was further angered and hurt to learn that George had talked to his sister about the issue for months before he finally confided in his mother.

Failing to find a successor, Paul Buttner eventually sold the business and retired. George now teaches English at an all-boys high school. And while he is content with his new career, George still carries feelings of guilt about his decision. And perhaps most unfortunate of all, today he and his father maintain a polite, but distant relationship, nothing like the times they'd spent together each fall in the woods, laughing and talking about nothing and everything.

ENDING THE TRADITION

George Buttner faced the very difficult choice of balancing his own career interests against the backdrop of obligation and loyalty to the family business. Certainly, Paul Buttner's hope—that his son would enter the business and become his successor—played to George's sense of duty. For many young adults, this strong sense of loyalty exists even when their parents have explicitly stated that there is *no* requirement for their children to enter the family business as employees. But young adults frequently impose this sense of responsibility on themselves. Family traditions can be powerful forces and maintaining a successful legacy is a daunting challenge. This is particularly poignant in the context of a long-term legacy and years of involvement with the family business. This was the case with George. He had spent his summers mowing the lawn around the business and had frequently been called on as a part-time employee, doing odd jobs for the company throughout his childhood. These were childhood ties that George was forced to sever.

Aside from a sense of responsibility and obligation to the family business, many young adults are interested in joining the family business because of natural opportunities for advancement within the company. These young adults sense that the family business will provide a much quicker route to key management positions than would be available if they sought employment on the outside. George Buttner originally saw the business as an opportunity for more flexibility in terms of his working conditions, schedule, vacation time and other benefits that come with being part of the owning family. In George's case, however, these attractions were undermined by the realization that he had no personal passion or commitment to a career in the outdoor sporting apparel industry. Instead, his perspective outside the family business showed George that his interests were quite different than those of his father and, to really find career satisfaction, he needed to follow his own passion.

The requirement that family members be employed outside of the family business early on gave George the opportunity to evaluate *his* interests, as opposed to fulfilling the ambitions of his father. George was able to find his path without having the tensions of the day-to-day interactions at the family business. "I would have made the decision to leave the family business someday, anyway," George confided. "It was hard, but I still believe it was better early on than later."

George, like many young adults in line to lead the family business, had to struggle not only with decisions all young people have about their careers but also the added pressure of having to leave the family business to find any alternatives. In that kind of a context, a career choice is made, but the decision becomes personalized. Rightly or wrongly, a decision to seek a different career may be interpreted as a decision to leave the family. As George's relationship with his father demonstrates to this day, the emotions and attachments to the family and its business are neither severed nor mended easily.

The Brockmeyer Family
When making Dad happy doesn't make her happy

The Brockmeyer Co., Inc. was a merger/acquisition specialist firm owned by Henry and Barbara Brockmeyer, their son, Jason, and daughter, Emily. Jason and Emily received their ownership through the stock gifting program that was part of the estate plan established by their parents.

Henry built the company after an early career in banking and, later, with a large consulting firm in New York City. Henry was the deal maker of the company; he had excellent communication skills and relied on his experience and knowledge of the marketplace for the success of the business.

Emily held an M.B.A. from Stanford and was highly competent in financial analysis and applying that analysis to each deal. She also interacted professionally with the clients.

Jason was a very successful stockbroker with a major brokerage firm in the same city as the family business. And while Jason enjoyed some of the financial benefits of his ownership and helped with some decisions regarding strategic issues and opportunities for the family business, he was not involved in the daily operations. Despite his fairly analytic capabilities, Jason had always been something of a free spirit, intent on pursing his own interests. A bachelor, he enjoyed the flexibility and freedom provided by his broker responsibilities, taking long weekends to pursue his love of bicycling. Because of issues concerning fairness and equity in the distribution of his parents' assets, however, Jason held an equal stake in the business with his sister.

Emily described her position to me as carrying out a family role in the business typical of many daughters. In addition to her business responsibilities, she served as the bridge between her mother and her father. Her father has been absorbed in the business for years and communication between her father and mother deteriorated over the years as well, often leading to serious misunderstandings. Emily found herself not only the caretaker of the business but the family interpreter and mediator as well. And while she did not say it directly, Emily was not happy with the various roles she played in these relationships. Now that she had her own family, with two children who needed her attention, she realized that the old dynamics with Mom and Dad had to change.

Emily had reached a point in life at which she needed to decide whether she was content forever being the family caretaker or if she wanted to assert herself and run the business her own way. While the gifting of shares in the company was initially appreciated by both children and understood as an important tax-planning strategy for their parents, it left Emily with the fear that her brother could threaten her investment of time and energy in the business. Jason would always have an equal voice in the business through his equal ownership in the business. And he would benefit financially from the success of the business, even though she had done all the work.

Emily's concerns were amplified when she learned that her parents were considering a divorce after thirty-five years of marriage. While Emily was close to her mother, she also worked daily with her father in the business. She realized that she had been thrust into the middle of her parents' marital problems. "It was an awful time," Emily said. "During the day, I'd hear one side of the story, then at night I'd talk to Mom and hear something else. I was being pulled in so many directions."

Henry and Barbara faced a common marital predicament for family business owners. The early years of their marriage had allowed Barbara to focus her time and attention on her children, while Henry spent all of his time with the demands of growing an entrepreneurial venture. Once the "empty nest" syndrome hit home, Barbara had hoped that she and Henry could have more time for vacations and world travel. Henry, however, was still a workaholic. Over the years, their interests had grown in opposite directions. Finally they realized that their marriage was more of a habit than a commitment. Of course, with marital property laws to consider, Henry and Barbara realized that their divorce might wreak havoc on the business.

Emily thought that the crisis instigated by the divorce would create an opportunity to re-evaluate the entire business structure and its future. She felt that since she, not her brother, had made the family business her career, she was the obvious choice for future majority ownership and an opportunity to purchase majority control of the business. She saw her parents' impending divorce as a chance to redirect her life. And while that was what Emily wanted, an enormous gap remained between her unspoken wishes and reality.

How could Emily assert her own needs and express her own concerns for the future while at the same time remain the unselfish emotional caretaker of the family, and the mediator between her mother and father? Emily was caught between being business manager and protecting her mother. She was the adult protecting the family business, and she was the child, protecting her mother. Her parents' impending divorce forced her to face the issue of her own adult development, and she needed to rethink her role in both the family and the business.

After consultation, Emily decided to move beyond her caretaker role. She recognized her only real choice was to make her needs known and to act on those needs. Otherwise she would remain in the child/protector role and her own growth would never take place. Emily expressed to the family her desire to purchase the business from her parents and run it herself. Her offer to purchase the business not only helped Emily meet her needs, but at the same time it provided liquidity for the divorce settlement.

Jason's response was not surprising. He saw her decision as a threat to his interests. He had been able to have his own career, enjoy his flexibility and lifestyle *and* be part of the family business. When Emily acted on her needs, she altered her relationship with both the business and her family.

Family dynamics and changing business structure often work in tandem with one another. Emily wanted to buy the business and control it herself. She also wanted to protect the future for her own children. She was torn between her competing roles as the mother to her own children, the president of the family business and the daughter to her parents. But she was plagued by guilt for leaving the caretaker role that she had maintained for so long. She found herself caught between the desire to have her own separate and independent adult autonomy and emotional dependence on her traditional family role.

And here is the paradox—not until she left her traditional role behind, could she have a truly adult relationship with her family. "To have what I really wanted, I had to take a searching look at myself," Emily said in one meeting. "I realized that I could drift along and be unhappy, or I could give my life direction and make my own choices. It was frightening, but I did it."

GROWING UP WHILE GROWING OLDER

With her history of being the emotional caretaker for much of the family, Emily found difficulty in asserting her own personal desires and needs. Coupled with the changing dynamics of her family and the development of her own career needs, Emily picked her way through one of the most turbulent times in her life. She began to understand the importance of effective communication, for both family and business issues.

In particular, Emily had fallen into a "Bermuda Triangle" regarding her relationship with her parents. Triangulation often occurs when conflict, anger, resentment or frustration has built up between two people. To alleviate this build-up, one of the people "downloads" the negative feelings by sharing them with a third party. This certainly happened with Emily in her relationship with her parents. She had become the go-between for her mother and father. Finally, her parents' difficulties erupted, resulting in divorce. However, Emily had already become a corner of the triangle. While Emily continued to facilitate indirect communication between her mother and father, the true issues the pair experienced—anger, frustration and resentment—were passed on from one person to the next. There were no positive efforts to address the real sources of tension. In order to become a self-suffi-cient, independent adult, Emily needed to break that negative cycle.

In addition to the communication dynamics within the family, Emily also faced common intergenerational issues concerning roles and relationships in the family business and her desire to own the company. For many siblings in family-owned businesses who have acquired equal stock ownership through gifting from parents, the issue becomes one of fairness. Those siblings active in the business may resent the financial benefits that accrue to their brothers and sisters who have not been active participants in the enterprise but benefit financially nevertheless. Parents want to be fair, but that fairness may create inherent problems for the successor generation.

Clearly, from Henry and Barbara's parental perspective, there was a need to treat both of their children equally in the distribution of their estate. From Emily's perspective, however, there was a need for the recognition of her ongoing contribution to the success of the business. It was appropriate for her brother to share equally in the successes created by their parents, but she felt that future growth and success of the business should be hers alone, because her brother did not have the same role or responsibility in the ongoing activities of the business. "I'm the one in there every day, doing the work and taking the business forward," Emily said. Her brother's response was common: "She gets a salary to do what she does. Isn't that fair compensation?"

The issues facing the Brockmeyers are fairly common, given the needs of senior and successor generations. The dynamics between the two generations change over time, a fact demonstrated, in particular, by research using The Family Business Assessment Tool™ (see the Preface for more information). While younger successors tend to rate the various aspects of their family business fairly positively, successors between ages of thirty-five and forty-five often give low ratings to their experiences—in fact, the lowest ratings of any one subgroup within a family business. Tension is caused by the difference in the needs of each generation: As the senior generation matures, they hope to harvest the business, but the successor generation is priming to reinvest in the future of the business for its growth and success.

Emily Brockmeyer experienced a re-evaluation of her life as she reached her mid-thirties, at the same time that her parents were going through a major transition in their own lives. In many family businesses, due to the difference in age between the senior and successor generations, members of the successor generation may be going through a major life transition at the same time that their parents are experiencing an equally challenging life transition. The Brockmeyers were each in a period of flux individually, and these coincided to create a fairly difficult set of circumstances to be resolved.

Realizing that there is a high probability for conflict during periods of time when both generations are in a period of instability and change, it serves families and businesses well if they anticipate potential future transitional points in their relationships and build some structures to account for these. For example, the Brockmeyers needed to develop a fairly clear path of succession and future ownership that was consistent with Emily's ongoing commitment to work in the business.

Many children of family business owners delay adulthood until their mid-thirties or even early forties as a result of working in a family business. The familial relationship of a son or daughter is carried into the business relationship, thus allowing successors to continue in a traditional role, postponing independence. In such cases, it can be either the child or the parent who has trouble evolving into new relationships. For the Brockmeyers, the family was willing to explore alternatives once Emily decided to be direct about the issues and her desire to one day own and run the business. For the Buttners, on the other hand, the father's agenda for the perpetuation of the family business legacy became an obstacle to supporting his son's alternative career interests.

Certainly, young adults need to acknowledge what they truly want to do with their lives, even if they don't fulfill their parents' hopes and plans. George Buttner may have never wanted to work in retail, but he was so locked into pleasing his father that he at first convinced himself it was what he wanted. Finally, after several years of work outside of the family business, George learned that his passions lay elsewhere. Emily Brockmeyer, traditionally playing the role of caretaker and mediator, finally reached her own adult decision to be more direct and to express her own needs.

In both cases honest, direct communications—while not easy— could have helped both families make the transitions they faced simpler. If George had been honest and discussed the issues openly, and if his father, Paul, had been more open-minded about his son's needs and not just his own, the family might have come to a solution without damage to the business or the family. Their different paths would have created a more harmonious family, even if a nonfamily president operated the business.

The Vierhaven Family
Flying solo when the plane is full

Carl Vierhaven was a shipbuilder in Holland twenty-five years ago, when he developed a specialized pump that met the needs of the marine market. He obtained a patent for the product, moved to the United States and continued to develop his business. The product flourished and soon every boat owner, from weekend sailors to ocean liner companies, used Vierhaven pumps and related products. Annual sales at Vierhaven Marine Ltd. reached more than $30 million.

Carl Vierhaven and his wife, Jenna, had two sons and a daughter. Their daughter graduated with honors from a prestigious law school and had a thriving practice as a patent attorney. The oldest son, Bob, grew up to become the company's chief engineer. But over several years in the business, Bob became increasingly frustrated with his father, who remained strong-minded about the way he wanted to run the business. One week after his thirty-sixth birthday, Bob decided he'd had enough of his father's autocratic management style and, to his father's surprise, he quit the family business. He gave a week's notice, moved to a different state and accepted a position designing electronic circuits at an aerospace manufacturing company.

Peter, Carl Vierhaven's second son, had attended college briefly, but then joined the company while still in his early twenties. Like his father, Peter was entrepreneurial and, while working at the family business, had started his own catalog parts distribution business for sailors, which he operated in his spare time. Peter's business did not compete with Vierhaven Marine. Carl Vierhaven, admiring Peter's entrepreneurial flair and his son's success at this independent business venture, gave Peter more management responsibility in the family business. It became obvious his father had begun to prepare Peter for succession.

Peter's business success, however, took significant time from his daily responsibilities at the company and, faced with his father's obvious plans, Peter felt he had to make a decision. Peter realized that in order to take a serious leadership role in the family business, he would have to drop his own business venture. He was torn between his desire to be part of the family legacy and his desire to be an entrepreneur in his own right. Peter also sensed that although his father wanted him to take over the company, Carl would still want to maintain control over day-to-day operations. Carl's controlling style was the issue that had driven Bob from the company. Peter was also frustrated with his father's style of business but, unlike Bob, decided to confront his father directly. "I knew if I didn't, there would be misery down the road," Peter said. "I decided now was the time to get it all on the table."

Peter agreed to accept his father's offer of the presidency but only if certain conditions were satisfied. Peter insisted his father could not interfere in day-to-day management. During the transitional period, people in the company would start to report to Peter and his father would eventually retire and leave the company. Peter also suggested that his wife run the distribution business, which they had developed together, as a subsidiary of Vierhaven Marine. Carl, who was still rebounding from his older son's departure, agreed to all the terms.

While Carl never changed his own style dramatically, his sons took very different approaches to dealing with him. When Peter was faced with a decision either to pursue his own interests or pursue the opportunities at the family business, rather than leave his job at Vierhaven Marine, Peter took action and confronted his father. Peter knew he had to express his own needs and make an attempt to change the environment his father had created. In doing this, Peter helped Carl realize that unless he changed his ways, he would lose a second successor.

Typical of many entrepreneurs, Carl Vierhaven was strong-willed, demanding and autocratic in his approach to the business. While Carl would delegate responsibilities to both of his sons working in the business, he had a tendency to interfere in each son's departmental duties, causing disruption by second-guessing the implementation plans and activities that each son had organized with the workers of their departments.

This style of autocratic control tended to put the senior generation in a position of parental authority in relationship to all employees in the company, following what one of my clients likes to call the "Golden Rule:" He who owns the gold, rules. Both Vierhaven sons, Bob and Peter, responded to these entrepreneurial leadership characteristics embodied in their father's management style, but dealt with the issues in different ways.

Both brothers felt that they needed to express their independence and their need for authority and accountability in their work relationships. For Bob, this meant leaving the family business in order to pursue opportunities in a different business environment, one where there was open, participatory management. Change also provided Bob with the opportunities he needed to grow independently and appreciate his own accomplishments.

Peter, on the other hand, had already established himself as a strong and independent leader with the business that he had developed separately from the family business. Stylistically, the personality traits of Peter were very similar to those of his father. Both father and son had strong entrepreneurial spirits and both were fairly decisive and aggressive in their business strategies.

While Bob chose to leave the business, Peter chose to assert his own boundaries and conditions for working in the family business. He made it clear that this was the only way to ensure family succession and multiple generation continuity. Peter Vierhaven chose to make his own decision about his role and involvement in the family business, and was willing to face the consequences if his father found those conditions unacceptable.

VICTIMS ARE THE ENEMY OF ACTION

Successors in family businesses often complain about the leadership style of their parents or the unwillingness of their parents to let go of decision making within the business. Both situations contribute to the creation of inadequate management opportunities for their children. Young adults will often act as victims, complaining that their parents won't let go, won't retire, micro-manage all situations, do not allow for active participation of the successors in decision making, and so forth. From an adult development standpoint, however, both Bob and his brother, Peter, were much more decisive about their management roles and succession opportunities within the company. Rather than merely complain about the situation or feel frustrated, both evaluated their own situations and made personal choices about the roles they would play in the company's future. Part of having adult relationships is the willingness not only to express personal needs and concerns but also to take responsibility for the consequences of the actions that follow. For Bob, this meant leaving the business and pursuing his own career on his own terms. For Peter, this meant establishing clear boundaries and guidelines for his roles and responsibilities in the business and holding his father accountable to these as part of the conditions of his continued employment.

BUILDING ADULT FOUNDATIONS

The four cases discussed in this chapter illustrate how the underlying critical issues for successful transitions within family businesses concern the establishment of adult relationships among family members. As children grow older, they must learn how to function as separate, independent, self-directed individuals in relation to their parents and the rest of their family. The key to having a successful transition from a family of children to a family of adults rests in the power and skill that the family has in using communication tools. Families who have difficulty making this transition tend to have undefined rules that maintain their existing structures and undermine open communication. In particular, the communication dynamics within families who have difficulty functioning together as adults fall into the following categories:

1. Fuzzy Boundaries

In dysfunctional families, where conflict abounds and communication is difficult, there is often a lack of clear boundaries that respect the alternative perspectives and feelings of various family members. In many cases, the family has grown up with a tradition that takes care of the needs of the parents, with little value seen in understanding the needs of the children, such as the need for privacy or the need to express feelings without retaliation. Family members are not allowed to express or even experience their own feelings, especially those that are unacceptable to their parents.

2. Triangulation

One of the most common dysfunctional relationships that can emerge in a family is triangulation. This occurs when one family member is caught in the middle of conflict between other family members, often a son or daughter between parents or among siblings. Although triangulation happens frequently, it is rarely effective in resolving the underlying issue. As mentioned when discussing Emily's relationship with her parents, triangulation involves communicating through a third party.

In most dysfunctional families, internal communication is usually directed through a son, daughter or sibling who attempts to mediate the tensions and disagreements between those family members having the conflict. As such, the third party functions as a defense against intimacy and honesty. To be effective, family members should speak directly to each other to resolve their conflicts.

3. Indirect Communication

Dysfunctional families typically discourage clear and direct communication about feelings. For example, if there is conflict and family members feel upset or angry, they are usually unable to share these feelings openly with other family members. Instead, they may express their angry feelings through such indirect means as innuendo, sarcasm, silence and withdrawal. As a result, dysfunctional families rarely have in-depth conversations with one another, and are unavailable to one another to talk about the feelings they have or the conflicts they might be experiencing. In entrepreneurial businesses, this dynamic of unavailability is further complicated by the intense focus on the business at the expense of the family.

4. Emotional Cutoff

In families where conflict and dysfunction run rampant, these implicit rules designed to discourage open communication are enforced through a process of emotional cutoff. If family members have feelings that they want to express, have a perspective that goes against the grain of the family, or want to assert their own needs when those are not consistent with those traditionally valued by the family, their punishment is to be excluded and disowned from the family. In family businesses, this penalty is often beyond an emotional penalty, where people who break the family rules are shunned. They may also be controlled financially by threats that they will be disinherited, or even sued, if they do anything to violate the goals, perspective and agenda of the dominant family member—usually, the entrepreneurial founder of the family business.

In contrast, successful families build strong foundations through open communication, not only among siblings but also between parents and their children. Positive communication patterns within healthy families tend to embody the following key elements:

1. Active Listening

Successful communication in a family business requires an active interest in listening to the needs of any and all family members. Such listening is sometimes referred to as "empathic listening." The power of empathic, active listening rests in really understanding the perspective of another person. Family members need to learn to listen to one another and to recognize that each family member needs the assurance that he or she has been understood. Such understanding builds personal confidence and a sense of self-worth. Successful entrepreneurs, however, often have not learned how to listen to others. They may be extremely good at being decisive and taking creative risks but not very skilled at listening to and understanding other people's needs and perspectives. Improvement in communication takes time, patience and conscious effort by all sides.

With practice, it is possible to learn to listen actively to other family members in order to gain an understanding of their feelings, needs and perspectives. Until people's positions are clearly understood, it is very difficult to negotiate or mediate a settlement that will allow as many people in the family as possible an opportunity to find a collaborative and cooperative solution to their conflicts.

2. Direct Communication

When Emily Brockmeyer was caught in the triangle of the conflicts and disagreements between her mother and father, she was dragged into their marital relationship. Communication triangles are very common in families, and are activated when anxiety, conflict or tension develops between two people who have an emotional relationship with one another. When the increase in anxiety disturbs the relationship between these two people, a third person, such as Emily, becomes involved in the tension of the twosome, attempting to decrease the anxiety in the twosome by spreading it through a three-person relationship.

Avoiding these destructive triangulation patterns will improve the communication patterns within a family. Rather than being dragged into a twosome's disagreement, it is more effective if the third party helps facilitate open communication, promoting and participating in empathic, active listening by the two parties. In other words, the third party can be involved in this process, but he or she should be involved to help improve the quality of the communication between the two parties that have the dispute, rather than as a safety net to avoid dealing with the issues between the two parties.

A third party must learn not to take sides, instead using all of his or her effort and resources to get the two people with a dispute to discuss what they feel they cannot discuss. This, however, requires that people understand the basic elements of effective mediation and negotiation.

CONFLICT RESOLUTION TECHNIQUES

Most conflicts occur in family businesses when the needs of one family member or group of family members are not being met sufficiently, usually because other family members' needs have been made the focus of attention. The mediation process identifies win/win situations in which the needs of all family members can be met adequately.

Healthy adult families prefer to find solutions that support and affirm the different needs of different family members. The challenge is to find practical solutions that do not sacrifice the needs of one family member at the expense of another family member.

To find solutions to these conflicting needs, the elements of collaborative and cooperative bargaining are, perhaps, the most helpful. The basic elements of such negotiation have been outlined succinctly by Fisher and Ury in their well-known book, *Getting to Yes*.[1] They recommend the following five steps as the basis of an effective resolution of conflicting needs:

---

1 From *Getting To Yes*, Second Edition, by Roger Fisher, William Ury and Bruce Patton. Copyright © 1981, 1991 by Roger Fisher and William Ury. Adapted and reprinted by permission of Houghton Mifflin Company. All rights reserved.

1. Separate Individuals From the Problem

Focus attention on the issues that need to be addressed, not on the personality characteristics or problems of the individuals involved. Work to fix the problem, not to fix the person.

2. Focus on Needs

Rather than focusing attention on individual *solutions* to the problem, focus on the underlying *needs* that must be met by the solutions. For example, George Buttner had a need to find a satisfying career. There may have been many solutions to meet this need, both within the family business and through careers outside the family business. Emily Brockmeyer had a need to be rewarded for her contribution to the ongoing growth and success of the business. Again, there are various solutions that could meet this need, one of which was to buy out her brother's ownership position in the company; another might have been to increase her salary and incentive program to compensate for her success in growing the business.

3. Identify Alternative Solutions

Rather than using the most immediately accessible solutions to the problem, work to investigate several alternative options that might address the needs of the individuals in the situation. It is often helpful to have outside perspectives, such as that provided by accountants or attorneys, or management consultants, who can present a range of alternative solutions that may not have been considered by the individual family members.

4. Focus on Objective Criteria For Resolving the Conflict

Beyond the needs of the individuals and their emotional reaction to these situations, make sure that you find objective criteria to identify alternatives for the different parties who have a conflict. For example, as Peter Vierhaven took over more of the leadership responsibilities in his father's business, objective criteria could be used to measure his success or failure of leadership, and thereby justify to what degree his father should have continued involvement in day-to-day decision making. Such objective criteria could include calculation of the return on investment that the business had achieved, or the ability of Peter to meet the predefined goals and objectives for sales growth in the business. Without objective criteria, it is very difficult to measure the success or failure of various solutions to the conflict.

5. Understand the Best-Alternative Solution

Finally, the parties in the conflict over needs in the family business need to understand their own best-alternative solution. One of my clients likes to refer to this as "drawing a line in the sand." After active listening, and after clearly defining alternatives, needs and potential solutions to a conflict, all of the parties must be quite clear about the degree to which they are willing to compromise or sacrifice some of their own needs in order to find a solution that benefits everyone. The reason most people will enter into a negotiated settlement over a conflict within a family business is that they believe they can obtain better results and more flexibility with a collaborative solution than in having a winner and a loser. In certain situations in a family business, however, there comes a point at which compromise cannot be reached and the individual parties need to decide where that line should be drawn in the sand.

Active listening, direct communication and conflict resolution are key elements of effective communication patterns in families that have achieved adult/adult relationships with one another. But how do families practice these techniques? How do they learn to implement open and effective communication patterns if those patterns have not been the standard model of the families' communication to date?

Many families run into situations where members feel they cannot discuss issues with one another. They avoid discussions to protect other family members, hoping to avoid conflict. For example, a sibling group might care so much about their father and his need to be active and involved in the business that they do not confront him with their concerns about the strategic direction of the company. Many families discover that these seemingly unspoken issues are, in fact, effectively discussed once they are shared among family members. The family, however, fears these issues because they do not know how to approach difficult topics in a sensitive way. Failure to discuss such issues often leads to greater conflicts and crises within the family.

If the family does not regularly use positive communication patterns, then it is critically important that the family involve an outside professional facilitator to help identify and improve underlying problems within the communication patterns of the family. The facilitator helps to make sure that all members of the family have an opportunity to express and articulate their perspectives. Then alternative positions are clearly identified so that all family members feel they have been understood and that their perspective and point of view has been included in the family discussion before particular solutions are decided as the best for the family.

Families in business must improve their communication techniques and learn more effective, adult-based relationship patterns *before* they tackle the most critical issues facing their family business. In these cases, the family must create an environment where family members identify, learn and practice more effective communication tools, building the skills and resources necessary to address the needs and concerns of each of the family members.

Questions to Discuss About Family Dynamics:

Families often develop rigid and unbreakable patterns that force them to repeat the same communication failures time and again. To move from dysfunctional patterns to healthy ones, a family must first recognize the individual needs of each family member as an adult. Trust must be established to serve as a safety net in order for the family to take the risks of open communication and negotiation to meet diverse needs. To explore these issues, discuss the following questions with your family:

+ Do members of the family feel comfortable sharing their alternative feelings and needs with one another, or is it too dangerous to really speak the truth?

+ Do family members know how to listen to one another, and do they understand the different needs of all the family members? Could you write a list of everyone's personal needs and how these differ?

+ Have family members found satisfying careers either within the family business or elsewhere, that provide a foundation for emotional and financial independence from the family?

+ Has your family established appropriate boundaries between the family and the business?

+ The Family Business Assessment Tool™ measures three success factors concerning family dynamics: Family culture, career satisfaction and family relationships. How would you rank your family on these factors?

MAKING
THE GRADE

Chapter 3

The transition to adulthood deals with the quality and nature of the relationships among family members. Beyond the interrelationships within the family, the relationship between the family and the business must also be clarified. For any family business, the entry of the next generation signals an important transition from a closely held entrepreneurial business to a family-owned, multigenerational business. But as family members of the successor generation reach the age where full-time employment makes sense, what should the family set as the standards and requirements for employment of family members? It is important for families to address family employment issues before problems and crises emerge.

Interpersonal relationships, as we saw in the last chapter, can either be defined on an adult-to-adult basis or be maintained on a parent-to-child basis. Families that make the commitment to develop and foster adult relationships transfer these strong family foundations to the way in which they manage their family business and relate to one another. Families that function together as adults learn to listen and balance the competing needs of different family members. Using a strong commitment to healthy adult communication patterns, one of the first tasks for families in business is to determine the ground rules for the interaction between the family and the business. Do you create job openings to accommodate family members when they are in need? Do family members have an inherent right to employment or should business criteria be used to screen family employment, just as employment criteria would be used in the hiring of nonfamily employees? Which should take priority in determining the employment of family members—business principles or bloodlines? Will you create a social welfare system of family entitlements or a business system based on competency, capabilities and the competitive demands of the marketplace? Families built on strong adult foundations choose business solutions to these critical issues.

The way your family answers these questions will set the tone for all the other family business employment issues that you will face. Not only do rules of entry for employment need to be established, but the general approach to understanding the relationship between the family and the business establishes the basis for promotions, career development and, ultimately, the selection of the future leaders of the business. Let's see how several different families have struggled with these issues, as they set the tone and agenda for their involvement as a family that owns and operates a business.

The Anders Family
All families are created equal

Anders, Inc. made packaging material for the health care industry. Philip Anders and his wife, Rita, owned the business and had four children, two daughters and two sons. Rita, a health care researcher, developed the products sold by their business. Philip was in charge of sales and marketing. With Rita's keen sense of the health care industry and Philip's expert sales experience, Anders, Inc. grew to be a $15 million business.

The Anders believed in establishing good communication within their marriage, as well as within the entire family, and both were committed to developing their children as responsible adults. They put into practice the communication techniques described in the last chapter. Early in their life as a family and as a business, they established a Family Council. Philip and Rita kept their children informed about the business through regular family meetings each quarter, even before the children graduated from high school. During the meetings, the parents hoped they could keep lines of communication open with their children, as well as teach them about the issues and dynamics of the business.

As the children grew older and finally became employed full time in the business, the regular family meeting structure provided a format for maintaining clear communication and open business discussions. Because these meetings were guided by an agenda and had a definite purpose, the family successfully created clear boundaries between family relationships and business issues. Everyone in the family knew, from years of experience with regular meetings, that the quarterly business meetings were the forums for the discussion of business issues and their impact on the family.

Consistent with their commitment to good communication within the family, Philip and Rita also established rules of entry to the company. The children needed to have a college education in something relevant to the company's product line and expertise, or they needed to demonstrate a talent that was relevant to the business. In addition to education and training, both children knew they would have to gain experience outside of the family business before they could even consider applying for a job. Finally, they knew that they would have to complete the regular employee application procedure and follow the same selection criteria as any other person seeking employment at Anders, Inc. In fact, if anything, the commitment of their parents to avoid nepotism made the criteria more stringent for family members. They also established a compensation framework for all positions at the company. The framework ensured that wages, bonuses and benefits that family members received were based on an analysis and study of comparable jobs within their industry and within the geographic region where they did business. Knowing these criteria in advance, three of the Anders children, two sons and one daughter, became involved in the business after each had worked at a different company following graduation from college. Later, two went on to pursue master's degree programs in business administration.

With three children now employed in the company, and doing very well, Rita and Philip realized that it was time to consciously plan for their own retirement as well as the ultimate goal of transferring the management of the business to their children. Following their commitment to family business discussions, the parents decided to include a discussion of their retirement needs as part of one of the regular quarterly family business meetings. The accounting firm for Anders, Inc. had recently suggested that in addition to the 401(k) plan that had been established years before, Rita and Philip should consider a deferred compensation plan as part of their retirement planning program. Owners of closely held companies have often failed to set aside enough money for their own retirement and, as a result, advisors often recommend deferred compensation plans.

Rita and Philip recognized that they had the power, as the owners of the business, to establish a deferred compensation plan that met their own needs. But to be consistent with their commitment to fostering adult relationships within the family, they knew they should handle their own financial needs in the broader context of the needs of the business and the ability of the business to function in the future. Instead of announcing their intentions after the fact, Philip and Rita took their deferred compensation proposal to the Family Council meeting and presented it for discussion by the family. Was the plan in the best interest of the business? What would the impact of their deferred compensation be on the business? These can be crucial questions, because these plans may negatively affect the cash flow and, in turn, opportunities for the children to reinvest corporate profits in the company. In fact, the key issue concerned whether the deferred compensation plan would be in the best interest of the company—a criterion consistent with years of a business-first philosophy. Philip and Rita practiced what they preached. They held themselves to the same standards that they wanted to foster in their children.

After considerable discussion and review within the Family Council, the deferred compensation plan was approved, but with provisions that would protect the business. First of all, the family members decided that it was critical that Rita and Philip have adequate financial resources for their retirement years. In addition to the qualified 401(k) plan, the business started funding an insurance program designed as a nonqualified retirement plan. Also, the family agreed to establish clear financial criteria for the deferred compensation plan that were tied to the profitability of the business.

ALL THE RIGHT MOVES

Philip and Rita Anders are an example of a very healthy and highly functioning couple whose commitment to developing adult-to-adult relationships among family members shaped the methods they used for operating their business. Through the establishment of a Family Council while their children were still young, the Anderses were able to find balance between the needs of the business and the needs of the family. But in many other family business situations, it is much more difficult and challenging to maintain a commitment to good business principles when the livelihood of family members depends on their continued employment in the family business. The McKenzie family struggled with this issue, which ultimately led to conflict among family members.

The McKenzie Family
For love or money

Kevin McKenzie owned a firm called McKenzie Designs that specialized in point-of-purchase displays. Kevin started the company after working in the advertising industry for about twenty years. His son, Mark, who had a strong background in computer technology, joined the family business after working for a computer consulting company for several years following his graduation from a technical engineering college. After his first two years at McKenzie Designs, Mark developed software solutions for the design function of the displays, which gave the company a clear competitive advantage in the marketplace, in particular the ability to customize the point-of-purchase displays much faster. With Mark's innovative talents and his father's salesmanship and market experience, McKenzie Designs was growing at a rate of 20 percent per year while improving its profitability.

Kevin also had three daughters, two of whom, Amy and Mary Jane, had minor roles in the company. One daughter worked as a customer service specialist and the other as an accounts payable clerk. In addition, both daughters had husbands who worked in the business in sales positions. The third daughter, Sally, was not involved in the business.

Unlike the Anders family, Kevin McKenzie and his family had never formalized the criteria for family employment in the business. Furthermore, they had not established a pattern of good communication among family members. In the early stages of the business, Kevin needed all the help he could get from family members to meet the growing demands of customers. But as the business grew, and it became necessary to hire talented workers and experienced managers, it was evident that some sort of criteria would have to be established to manage the performance and growth opportunities for family members within the business.

As the sales force grew and new salespeople were added, the sons-in-law, Jim and David, consistently were ranked at the bottom of the sales force, in their abilities to both develop their own accounts and meet minimum quotas on house accounts. Their sales volume barely covered their salaries. Kevin was caught in a dilemma. He recognized the critical role that his son, Mark, had played in the growth of the business. But Kevin also felt a strong obligation to continue employing Jim and David, since their families, including his daughters and grandchildren, depended on the income they received from the business.

Based on Mark's critical role in developing the software that gave the company a competitive advantage, as well Mark's demonstrated commitment to the company, Kevin decided that Mark should be groomed for the presidency. Consequently, Kevin developed an estate plan that would give Mark voting control of the corporation at his death. In addition, he set up a "second-to-die" life insurance program that would provide additional financial resources to pay estate taxes. Kevin was comfortable with this decision to transfer control to Mark, since he felt the decision was based on Mark's contributions and that the company was in a much better position financially because of his son. Kevin, like most owners of closely held companies, wanted the business to continue and be controlled by a member of the family.

Kevin McKenzie's daughters, Amy and Mary Jane, were deeply concerned about this decision. While they recognized the contribution of their brother, they also knew that their father had always protected the family. They were not as confident that their brother would make family considerations a priority. They were right: Mark felt no familial obligation to protect his sisters and their families.

From the sisters' perspective, all family members had made contributions to the business, to the best of their ability. They and their husbands had been involved in the business as it struggled and grew in its early stages and they felt some entitlement to participate in the future success of the company.

Kevin McKenzie had often told the family that his hard work and effort to develop this business had been done "for the benefit of the family." His daughters knew that their father would protect family members and had made a commitment to employ any family member who wanted to work in the company. His daughters also were quite aware that their brother was much more likely to see the situation differently. Mark did not have the same kind of personal commitment to his sisters that their father had to them as his daughters. For many years, Mark was frustrated and complained about what he saw as the poor performance of his brothers-in-law. Although the daughters disagreed with their father's decision to slot Mark as the future president of the business and to give Mark future voting control of the company, they accepted their father's decision. Kevin continued to employ Jim and David, even though they were below average performers for the sales group.

With Kevin McKenzie's premature death, however, the family was thrown into turmoil. Kevin's vision of the family business as an opportunity for all family members to participate was lost under Mark's style of leadership. After his father's death, Mark took over as president. Now, with full control, Mark decided to establish clear sales criteria for all salespersons, including David and Jim.

Mark hired a nonfamily manager to be vice-president of sales. At a sales meeting, the vice-president challenged the brothers-in-law to improve their performance. Jim refused to listen to the new demands, threatening to quit if he was forced to attain new quotas. The new vice-president, backed by Mark, reinforced the sales quota requirements. Jim quit that afternoon. He came back the next day hoping to salvage his job, but Mark sided with the vice-president of sales and said his own credibility would be undermined if he rehired him. Jim was left without a job.

Amy and Mary Jane went to their mother, who had agreed with her late husband that Mark would become president. While she respected her husband's business choice and recognized Mark's clear contribution to the business and his business capabilities, she also wanted to protect her daughters and their husbands. Mrs. McKenzie was outraged when her son supported the termination of her son-in-law. "I was never so angry," she said, "as when Mark turned his back on the family. I felt we lost so much more than just Jim. I felt I'd never get my family back."

Mark's support of the vice-president of sales also outraged the sisters, who could not believe their brother would deny Jim a job and ultimately undermine the family. The mother, devastated by the conflict, began to push for family solutions, which meant rehiring Jim. Mark, however, refused to change his position in spite of pressure from the family. Mark stood by his vice-president.

RULES ARE MADE TO BE BROKEN

The McKenzies learned a painful lesson: A business cannot be run under two separate sets of standards—one for the family employees and one for all other employees. Ultimately, nepotism can destroy both the family and the business. Kevin McKenzie was willing to protect his sons-in-law for the sake of family harmony and to support his daughters and their children. Mark believed that the business had to be based on sound business criteria in order to remain competitive. Kevin's failure, however, was rooted in the fact that the family had not created a strong foundation for adult-to-adult communication. To function on a strong business foundation, the family must also be committed to a strong adult foundation—then both family harmony and business success can be achieved. To prevent this type of conflict, Kevin McKenzie should have identified clear rules of entry for any family member who wanted to work for the company. You cannot have employees, whether they are family members or not, who do not perform.

While his sons-in-law fit into the business environment in its early stages of the company's development, they failed to grow and expand their skills as the business grew. As talented and experienced outside salespeople began to be hired, David and Jim fell far behind in their ability to meet the needs and expectations of the company. Worse, the two had fallen into an attitude of entitlement. At the same time, their father-in-law, while he recognized their poor performance, was unwilling to take any action that might have disrupted harmony and goodwill within the family.

This is a common problem faced by owners of family businesses. The Anderses resolved this problem by setting clear guidelines for employment before their children had even graduated from high school. Thus for the Anderses, all family members understood the game plan for the business; there were no false hopes and no false expectations. The rules were clear to everyone.

In addition, the Anderses enforced this business philosophy in all aspects and dimensions of the family's interaction with the business, including the approach they took toward their own deferred compensation plan.

Kevin McKenzie, on the other hand, wanted the best of both worlds. He wanted to protect his family and provide as many benefits as possible to those he loved. By failing to establish employment criteria and failing to use good business practices in determining the growth, development and advancement of family members, Kevin's commitment to the family finally backfired. The eventual result was extensive conflict and turmoil among family members. After years of protection, the family was torn apart when Mark forced business-based criteria on the company.

Many see this issue as a choice between the family and the business. But by establishing adult responsibility and open communication, the Anderses demonstrated that a healthy family can operate a company using solid business criteria.

Dysfunctional families, with histories of codependency and entitlement, however, run the risk of destroying both the family and the business when they have to make choices about family employment.

FAMILY SERVES THE BUSINESS

When the question of choosing priorities comes up, clearly the health of the business must be paramount to family needs. If the business fails, *no* family member can benefit. The family should serve the business, rather than having the business exist simply to serve the needs of the family. And yet, many entrepreneurial founders feel a need to pass their success on to their children, whether the children are suited to the business or not. As one client said, "The hardest thing to see and to accept is the shortcomings of your own children." For many family business owners, this is an emotional no man's land.

For the McKenzies, two sets of standards where operating simultaneously. Clearly, Mark's promotion to the presidency was based on good business criteria. Mark demonstrated that he had the technical expertise, the commitment and the business knowledge to gain the respect of the other key managers. His brothers-in-law, however, had maintained employment based on their family membership, not their sales abilities.

Successful family-owned companies refuse to sacrifice their business to nepotism. They set criteria for both the initial employment and future advancement of family members by establishing rules of entry and making sure people are qualified for their jobs. It is much easier to work together to define the rules of the business game when a family has learned to function together as adults, when each family member has his or her own emotional integrity and self-sufficiency and each is willing to take on appropriate responsibilities. Without such adult development, families use the advantages of nepotism to perpetuate irresponsible dependency on the family and on the business. The dangerous and destructive nature of nepotism, coupled with dysfunctional family systems and the lack of adult development, create an imbalance in the interaction between work and the family. The Monnet family faced this crisis head on.

The Monnet Family
Making the best choice

Sebastian Monnet owned a small but profitable tool and die manufacturing company. He had two sons, Charlie and Samuel, who worked in the business and a daughter, Barbara, who was an attorney and had no interest in the business. Both sons held sales positions in the company and had worked in that capacity since they graduated from college. At ages twenty-four and twenty-six, respectively, Sam and Charlie each had only a few years of experience in the tool and die business. While Sebastian had set some general sales goals for each of his sons, they rarely met the targets and the sales they did achieve were based on the company's good reputation and long-term relationships with customers. Neither Sam nor Charlie had developed any significant new customers. Although sales should have been steadily increasing, they were flat for more than two years, and Sebastian became concerned.

Sebastian approached his sons and told them he felt they were not doing enough to encourage sales growth for the company. Both pointed to the fact that sales had not dropped in the years they were working for the company, although they had not increased either. Sebastian was extremely frustrated by his sons' nonchalant attitude. On the one hand, he wanted to fire both of them for their nonstellar performance and lack of concern. If they had not been part of the family, he certainly might have terminated them over a year earlier. As their father, however, he continued to hope that they would improve in their sales performance, getting "fired up" and excited about their jobs and increasing sales. When the situation did not improve after another year, Sebastian finally decided that he should establish sales criteria to measure each son's performance.

Sam and Charlie's personal lives contributed to their situations at work. They were both single and still lived at home. Their mother was doing all of their laundry, plus cleaning house and cooking for them. In addition to providing their employment and a base salary, the company also provided each with a new company car every two years. With all of their expenses paid for, room and board provided by their parents, cars provided by the company plus a base salary, each son had an extremely pleasant lifestyle that came without exerting much effort. It was obvious that no incentives would motivate the sons, since the family was already providing everything they needed. Rather than a sales incentive program, the parents needed to set some standards and expectations for their sons' continued employment in the family business.

The Monnets, in an effort to provide for their sons, had, in fact, created a system of entitlement. Their sons, used to being cared for by their parents, had never taken the appropriate steps to become separate and independent adults who could live on their own. The Monnets were meeting the needs of their sons at the expense of the needs of the business—and more importantly, at the expense of their sons' development as self-sufficient and responsible adults. In addition, the family had failed to develop an adult foundation for their relationships and responsibilities—they were still parents with children, and the parents were continuing a pattern that maintained the children's dependence on the family rather than establishing their own independence as responsible adults.

From a business perspective, Sebastian's decision to establish criteria to manage the employment of his sons was a step in the right direction. However, the Monnets faced a much deeper problem that was underlying their poor business performance. This deeper problem was rooted in the dynamics of their family and their failure to establish adult criteria for their interactions with one another. The children needed to move out of their family home—after all, they were twenty-four and twenty-six years old—and find work experience outside the family business. In that setting, they could establish their own emotional and financial independence from their parents.

As it turned out, Sebastian was reluctant to make any changes in the employment guidelines for his sons, in part to compensate for his own feelings of guilt. Sebastian was involved with a woman at the company, and the sons knew about it. To compensate for his guilt, Sebastian was letting the sons continue to work at a modest pace and yet be compensated well beyond what they deserved. The sons both felt they couldn't confront their father because he paid them well and indirectly paid all their expenses.

Clearly this was a family that had made no attempt to relate as adults, and the business reflected the dysfunctional aspects of the family. The mother was very attached to the children and reluctant to let them leave home. The father was irresponsible and unfaithful to his wife, violating her needs as well as the needs of his children. For the sake of keeping peace in the family, all members were reluctant to change their roles or confront larger, personal issues.

To resolve these issues, the Monnets needed to face the reality of the relationships they had created, both in their family and in their business. Sebastian had to face up to his infidelity, which eventually led to a divorce. The two sons had to move out of the security of their family home and become responsible for their own success or failure as adults. The company needed to establish clear criteria for sales performance and hold the Monnet children accountable to the same standards as their nonfamily salespeople.

ONE HAND NEEDS TO WASH THE OTHER

Unlike the Anders family, who developed open communication and created a Family Council for ongoing discussion of the issues where the family interfaced with the business, the McKenzies struggled with these issues. They tried to bring some balance between a sense of duty and responsibility to family members' needs and the growing demands of their business. The need to become more professional in how the business and the family members approached the market became vividly apparent. But for the McKenzies, the interaction between the family and the business reached a crisis point when Mark, the new president after his father's death, established business criteria as the foundation for their family business expectations. The change was traumatic. The Monnets, on the other hand, were dysfunctional both in their family *and* in their business.

These cases illustrate that a strong business philosophy, carried out by a strong and healthy adult family, creates a very positive family business strategy. In fact, research based on The Family Business Assessment Tool™ (see the Preface for more information) supports the direct correlation between family culture and business structure. If a family is functioning as an adult family, then obligations, responsibilities and accountability define their relationships with one another within the family. These same principles apply in the business. A healthy and well-functioning family is consistent with a well-functioning business.

These case studies—the Anderses, the McKenzies and the Monnets—all involve the tension and dynamics that may develop within a family when its members work together in the family business. In a sense, these three cases illustrate different stages of development along a continuum of the interaction between the family and the business. The Anderses, unlike the Monnets or the McKenzies, worked consistently to establish strong adult criteria for all the family members. At the other extreme, the Monnets illustrate a family where neither the parents nor the adult children were functioning as adults or taking responsibility for their actions and behaviors.

Yet whether a success or failure, *none* of these families took a critical step in bringing their companies up to a truly professional level. None of them had pulled together an outside board of directors, which would be able to provide business experience and objective criteria for running the business as well as deal with the critical issues concerning the family and the company.

The Hetzel family, as we will see, *did* take the steps needed to bring professional expertise into the company, but only after it became evident that a series of critical issues needed to be addressed. The growth of the business and the fact that the successor generation was ready to become employed in the family business forced this change.

The Hetzel Family
Forecasting can avoid the storm

The Hetzel family owns PetNet, Inc., a company that manufactures accessories for the pet industry, with a particular emphasis on bird owners. The company was founded more than one hundred years ago as a mill providing feed for poultry. Three brothers own the business: Irvin, Fred and Arthur Hetzel.

Although Irvin and Fred were very capable in their respective roles as operations manager and sales manager, the youngest brother, Arthur, was not as skilled. Even as head of human resources and administration, Arthur had really been supported in that role by the other brothers for twenty years. Arthur's department, while important to the business, was not the make-or-break function that accounted for business success at PetNet. Sales and operations were the cornerstones on which the business grew. However, as the business grew, Arthur's areas of responsibility became increasingly significant, particularly in keeping up with federal employment guidelines, since the workforce had now surpassed one hundred people. But just as important, if not more so, was the need for an efficient and effective accounting function that could keep pace with company growth.

Recognizing that their business was growing in complexity and that their children were graduating from high school and beginning to inquire about future opportunities in the business, Irvin, Fred and Arthur realized that they needed to formalize criteria for the family's involvement in the business. To do this, they decided to establish a formal, outside board of directors.

Irvin had three children, Fred had two and Arthur had six. Arthur's children were the oldest of the group, and two of them were hoping to join the company within a year or two. The brothers realized that problems could quickly arise, and wanted to establish criteria, or rules of entry, so that when the eleven nieces and nephews started knocking on the door, there would be qualifications each must meet in order to be hired. Not only did the brothers want rules of entry, they also wanted to establish compensation guidelines based on good business practices rather than family lineage. Cousins would not be paid based on family history but rather on their contribution to the business. In short, the Hetzel brothers wanted a compensation system based on performance, qualification and education.

After considerable discussion, the brothers, led by Fred and Irvin, decided to establish an outside board of directors. One of the functions of the board was to administer the criteria for employment and compensation to which they all had agreed. The board was comprised of the three brothers plus two outside board members who were successful presidents of their own companies. One of the first activities of the new board was to create a Family Business Plan for the company.

As the years went by, several of the cousins attempted to enter the business, but only one met the criteria established by the board. By setting up the criteria and following it, the board was building a foundation for the company's ongoing growth and success. Seven years after the new process was in place, one of Irvin's daughters, Irene, decided to apply for a position at the company. She met all the criteria, having completed her college education and having been successfully employed in an industry that had characteristics similar to the family business.

Because she knew about the rules of entry and understood the role of the board in the decisions concerning family employment, she wrote a letter to the board of directors and submitted her application for a position that was available. Irene followed the procedures for family employment, and was eventually hired for the position. There was no animosity from the other cousins who had been rejected for positions, because they knew she had successfully fulfilled the guidelines set out by their uncles and father several years earlier. The family had agreed upon an approach to family employment, had established a method for screening and interviewing candidates and, finally, had empowered their board of directors to carry out the plan.

MAKE A PLAN, STAY THE COURSE

The Anders family and the Hetzel family both created formal processes for the discussion of and development of key guidelines and criteria for the interface between the family and the business. For the Anderses, this developed through a Family Council, made up of just family members. The Family Council represents a family-centered approach to resolving the issues of the interface between the family and the business.

The Anderses business was successful, in part, because the parents established a strong commitment to the adult development of their children and open communication practices that, in turn, allowed each family member to be heard, understood and respected. The Hetzels, on the other hand, took a fairly business-centered approach to resolving these issues by forming an effective board of directors with outside, nonfamily members to bring a strong business perspective and objective set of standards to the operation of their business. The use of a Family Council, coupled with the use of a board of directors, is perhaps the most effective way to deal with family dynamics as they have an impact on business performance and vice versa.

A FAMILY COUNCIL

Many family business consultants recommend that families form a Family Council, with regular, structured meetings. This becomes a place where family members can discuss issues openly with one another, share their differences and find solutions *before* issues develop into full-blown crises.

A typical Family Council may include all of the family members who are stakeholders in the family and in the business. Participants may include active and inactive children (that is, those not employed in the business), as well as spouses, parents and other members of the extended family. The Family Council includes any family member who has an impact on the business and who, in turn, finds that the business has an impact on his or her personal and family life. Of course, large, multigeneration businesses with multiple family owners often restrict membership to only elected representatives from each branch of the family.

The success of the Family Council lies in the formulation of an otherwise informal exchange of viewpoints among family members. It is an excellent vehicle for sharing and exploring individual plans, long-term family goals and strategic business issues, as well as topics that affect sibling relationships, intergenerational dynamics and the relationship of family members to the business.

Brad, a newly appointed chief operating officer of his family's business, looked at it this way: "At first I resented the Family Council a little. I thought it would hold me back as I tried to expand the business. But later on I realized it did two things—it brought me face-to-face with my shareholders and face-to-face with all of my family."

Of course, a Family Council can be disastrous if the family is plagued by dysfunctional communication patterns. Families that do not understand the techniques of active listening and recognizing differences based on personality temperament, and who are not comfortable using general techniques of mediation and negotiation, would be well advised to consider using outside professionals to help facilitate their communication dynamics (see Chapter 2 for a detailed discussion of effective communication techniques). The facilitator's presence typically produces more effective family meetings.

The facilitator ensures that all members of the family have an opportunity to express and articulate their views, and that alternative positions are clearly identified. The result should be to give each family member a feeling of being understood, as well as a sense that their perspective and point of view were included in the family discussion before particular decisions were made.

There are several steps you should take to develop your own Family Council. Here are some that have worked for my clients:

1. Hire an Experienced Facilitator/Consultant

A family business facilitator combines excellent communication skills, meeting facilitation experience, business knowledge and, finally, an understanding of the legal dynamics affecting family business transitions. The consultant will make sure that the planning moves forward effectively and will mediate the differences in perspective among the various family members.

2. Identify the Participants

Clearly, family members should participate and, when a business is owned by more than one family unit, representatives from each branch of the family should be involved. The most frequent question that most families struggle with is whether or not to invite in-laws into these family business discussions. Often, the in-laws are restricted from owning stock. In my judgment, it is better to be inclusive rather than exclusive. In-laws should participate in these meetings unless there are clear, impending marital problems that might lead to divorce.

3. Attend a Seminar

For most family businesses, the transition between the generations is a new event—it has not happened before. That means there is no framework for understanding success or failure based upon past experience. Since it is important for families to obtain a broad-based overview of the most common strategies for building successful family businesses, I encourage families to become educated on family business issues. That way the family builds its own Family Business Plan based upon a strong foundation learned from the success of other family businesses. Some families hold a private seminar just for their own family members. Others attend educational programs offered by universities. Still others attend seminars and presentations prepared by their bank, accounting firm, law firm and family business consulting firm. Participate in such a seminar before diving into the details of developing your own Family Business Plan.

70

4. Identify Issues for Discussion

Most families would like to develop a Family Business Plan, and want to discuss the issues that are most significant to their family, but don't know where to begin. The Family Business Assessment Tool™ (see the Preface for more information) provides a series of questions dealing with a wide range of topics critical to the life of a family business. I use the Assessment Tool to identify similarities and differences between various members of the family in order to pinpoint which topics will be most critical for discussion at Family Council meetings. As a follow-up to gathering this initial information, it is also wise to interview individual family members to better understand their needs and concerns prior to starting a series of formal family meetings.

5. Develop Employment Guidelines

Very few family businesses establish formal guidelines for the employment and advancement of family members in the business, yet they are essential. Your employment guidelines should define criteria for hiring family members on a full-time basis. In addition, the family must determine what kinds of accountability and performance standards will be used to measure the growth and success of family members as they develop in positions within the company. Finally, the family must address issues about compensation. Will compensation be equal for all family members or will compensation be based on the fair market value of the position, as determined by industry or regionally based surveys?

6. Determine the Management Succession of the Business

In many respects, management succession and retirement planning for the senior generation are more complicated than estate planning, which is defined by federal tax requirements. Your family must answer several critical questions: Will a nonfamily president serve as a transitional bridge between the senior and successor generations? Will a formal board of directors be empowered to oversee the selection of the executive leadership of the company? Assuming talent and experience within the successor generation, will family members active in the business purchase the company as a retirement strategy of the senior generation?

Perhaps one of the most important questions a family must answer is: Will the successor group operate the business for its own benefit, taking over the entrepreneurial spirit that drives future growth? Or will the successors primarily serve a custodial role in managing the business for the benefit of all family members?

7. Establish a Method for Decision Making

When making the transition from the first generation to the second, most family businesses also make a transition from a kingdom to a democracy. But usually, families fail to establish a new form of corporate governance that allows the business to operate successfully with a group of owning partners—namely the sibling or cousin group (see Chapter 1 for examples and discussion of family business situations that struggled through this transition). How will decisions be reached when there are multiple owners with diverse interests and needs? Does someone have voting control? Or, will there be formal stockholder meetings to make key corporate decisions? What process will be used for resolving conflicts? Will you establish a board of directors empowered to protect the interests and needs of various stockholder groups?

8. Develop a Buy-Sell Agreement

Many buy-sell agreements are designed to minimize estate tax exposure when stock is gifted to the successor generation. While these agreements deal with government regulations, they often fail to establish fair and equitable guidelines for the buying and selling of stock among the active and inactive shareholders after the death of their parents. As soon as stock is gifted to the next generation, or whenever there are multiple shareholders, buy-sell agreements are a requirement. Buy-sell agreements should include a method for valuing the stock, terms for the purchase of stock and restrictions concerning ownership of stock, as well as triggering events—such as death, disability and retirement—that put the buy-sell agreement into action (see Chapter 6 for a discussion of estate planning issues and buy-sell agreements).

By establishing a Family Council and holding a series of meetings to discuss the broad implications and responsibilities of a family business, promises can be made that will not need to be broken. The formalized Family Business Plan will clarify the promises that family members make to one another and will serve as a road map to follow concerning the interaction between the family and the business.

9. Hold Your First Family Business Meeting

At the first meeting, the family should share its expectations, hopes and desires for the development of the Family Business Plan. This first meeting should set the stage for open communication and establish some ground rules for listening to one another and creating an atmosphere for open communication. During this meeting, the family should work on its Mission Statement. Discussion issues must include:

+ Why are we a family? Why are we in business?
+ What are the values we hold as a family?
+ What are the values we hold as a business that account for our success?

Finally—and perhaps most important—the family must determine whether it will operate the business for the benefit of the family or whether the primary purpose is for the family to serve the business. Will business criteria or family criteria be applied to make decisions that impact the employment, management and ownership of the family's business in the future?

Whether in a Family Council format or with a formal board of directors, one of the most critical steps that families in business must take is to establish guidelines and principles for the operation of the business and its interaction with the family.

Questions to Discuss About Family Employment:

This chapter emphasizes the importance of establishing a Family Council as a method to define the boundaries and relationships between the family and the business. Establishing guidelines for the employment and promotion of family members is one of the many responsibilities of an effective Family Council. At your next Family Council meeting, discuss these questions:

+ Have successors in the business established a level of emotional maturity that prepares them for business leadership?

+ Have successors mastered the technical and professional skills necessary to be effective contributors to the business?

+ Has your family business determined the requirements for the employment of family members? Explain.

+ Do you hold regular Family Council meetings? If not, how is the family kept informed about the business and its interface with the family?

+ Does your business operate under the "family first" or "business first" philosophy? How is this philosophy reflected in your family compensation guidelines?

+ The Family Business Assessment Tool™ measures three success factors concerning family employment: Successor development, successor competency and compensation standards. How would you rank your family on these factors?

GROWING PAINS

Chapter 4

I n our post-industrial age of information, families in business face a set of issues very similar to those found in the age of agriculture: How do we feed the growing family when the farm resources are limited by the available land? As Thomas Malthus[1] observed at the end of the eighteenth century, family population grows geometrically, and therefore more rapidly, than arable farmland, which grows arithmetically. Of course, modern farming techniques have increased yield tremendously, but not enough to deal with the geometric increase in the number of family members dependent on the family enterprise.

---

1 Thomas Malthus, *An Essay on the Principle of Population, as it Affects the Future Improvement of Society with Remarks on the Speculations of Mr. Godwin, M. Condorcet, and Other Writers.* (London: Printed for J. Johnson, in St. Paul's Churchyard, 1798).

When the farm started, it was most likely big enough to feed the mother and father and four children. But if the children grow up and have several children of their own, that same farm, with the same acreage, livestock and harvest, must be able to feed upwards of eighteen people or more. From providing for six people to as many as eighteen people is a tremendous increase, and it becomes obvious that the farm cannot stay the same size to continue to support all of those people. Either the family must acquire more land and livestock, or family members need to move off the farm. In agriculturally based societies, such as feudal Europe, leaving the farm to the eldest son solved the problem of succession.

So the growth and expansion of the family through marriage and birth becomes a critical issue in family businesses because it represents a classic struggle. At the same time that the successor generation is raising its own growing family, the senior generation is at an age when it does not want to risk financial assets. But in order to accommodate the growth of the family, the family business must grow as well, which means risk. To feed all the spouses and grandchildren in agrarian times meant adding more cows, chickens and land. In the post-industrial age of information it means building a new facility, hiring more salespeople or acquiring another business. These are risks that the senior generation often does not want to take.

The successor generation, on the other hand, realizes that the resources of the family farm or business must either expand to feed more members of the family or some family members need to move on. To grow, however, takes capital—capital that is usually owned and controlled by the senior generation. To balance the needs of the family with the needs of the business, the company must plan for the future.

For success, the whole family must take into account the growing demands of all the family members. Either the business must grow in both size and profitability, or fewer family members can plan to derive their income from the business. While all businesses need to develop a plan to compete in the marketplace, family businesses must also integrate the business plan with the ever-changing needs of the family.

For any company, developing a business plan is essential to its long-term survival. As the road map for the company, a business plan provides the direction that helps avoid roadblocks by regional, domestic and foreign competition; economic setbacks; and internal turmoil. As a business grows from its early stages into a viable company, a plan must be established that allows the company to compete effectively in the marketplace and provide adequate returns on investment. Clear business plans outline corporate goals and objectives and give employees, as well as managers, an essential reference point. For family businesses, the strategic business plan must address four major issues:

+ Corporate growth
+ Management development
+ Strategic positioning in the market place
+ Division of responsibilities through clear roles and responsibilities

The Chadwick family dealt effectively with the first of these major issues by determining the best way to grow the company, while at the same time being sensitive to the financial needs of both the family and the business.

The Chadwick Family
When needs differ, but goals are the same

The Chadwick family owned a marketing company that customizes products for promotional uses, such as water bottles, pens and umbrellas that are emblazoned with a company's logo. Bob Chadwick was a World War II veteran with an eye toward consumer growth. After several failed ventures, he found success with his own specialty advertising firm. Like many entrepreneurs, Bob Chadwick reinvested his profits in the company year after year, with current annual sales nearing $18 million.

Bob and his wife, Delores, had three daughters and two sons. All of the daughters, two sons-in-law and one son worked in the business. Despite its success, the company became strained financially, with all seven family members and two in-laws dependent on Chadwick, Inc., for their livelihood. And as the children's families grew through the birth of grandchildren, the extended Chadwick family continued to become more and more dependent on the financial success of the business.

Bob recognized that the family had two options—either fewer family members could work at the business or the business had to grow not only its sales but its profitability by focusing on the products with the largest margins. Simply put, Bob recognized that the demands of family salaries and benefits were a large portion of the overhead cost of running the company. As with many family businesses, there was a strong commitment to protecting the family and to providing employment for all family members who were interested in working at Chadwick, Inc. Therefore a strategy for growth was the preferred option for the company. However, such growth would require more capital—and capital required all family members to tighten their belts, take salary reductions and, finally, turn to the banks for financing expansion plans.

In the past, Bob and his wife, Delores, had financed business growth internally by reinvesting profits in equipment, building space and marketing efforts. But if the business was to support the multigenerational family, the growth necessary far exceeded the business' ability to generate sufficient capital. Chadwick, Inc. needed bank loans to buy new equipment, expand the building and hire new people. The bank, however, wanted personal guarantees from Bob and his wife. The couple, in their late sixties, did not want to put any more of their personal assets on the line. Bob and Delores, in fact, wanted to reduce their personal liability, take fewer risks and build a nest egg for their upcoming retirement.

"This was a crossroads for us," Bob explained one day in his office. "Delores and I built this for our children and for us. Were we being selfish by wanting to protect our share of the business?"

Many family business owners face this dilemma—they want to maintain the family business for future generations, but doing so means taking risks. This takes place right at the time they are ready to pull back and reap the benefits of the time, energy and money invested over the years.

As a solution to this seeming dilemma, Bob and Delores implemented a long-range estate plan. The couple split the ownership of the building from the operating company and started an aggressive gifting program of the company stock to the children. They hoped to thereby shift the future growth of the company to the children and minimize their federal estate tax exposure. In addition, they decided to secure a long-term lease of the building back to the business to provide regular monthly payments to support their retirement years (see Chapter 5 for a more detailed discussion of retirement strategies and Chapter 6 for more discussion of estate planning strategies). Perhaps most important, the children, who now owned stock in the company, were asked to share in the financial needs of the business by placing some of their own assets at risk.

Bob and Delores's son Randy was named president and immediately started planning for growth based on new technologies and increased marketing efforts. Randy wanted to purchase computer technology to automate the business so it could operate faster and more efficiently. He also wanted his sales department, which included his two brothers-in-law, to begin an aggressive marketing and sales campaign that required from them large time commitments and increased travel. Through strategic planning meetings that included the employed family members as well as key nonfamily managers, the management team developed a thorough plan based on niche market sales tactics. Each family member, as well as each manager, had specific actions to carry out to make sure the plan was successfully implemented. With a well-thought-out business plan, it was much easier to obtain bank financing in support of the growth objectives.

Through these successful efforts the business grew at a rate that could financially support the growing family needs, repay the bank loans and maintain the lease payments on the building for the parents' retirement income. As an added benefit, because the ownership of the business was gradually transferred to the successor generation, the successful growth in the equity value of the business occurred in the estates of the successors rather than the parents. Thus, that growth in equity was not included in the parents' estate for tax purposes.

LOOKING AT BOTH SIDES OF THE COIN

The Chadwicks' plan to expand the business to meet the needs of their growing family worked. Their estate planning decisions allowed the growth to accumulate in the estates of their children rather than in their own estate. But all the family members had to work together to implement this growth strategy—they had to accept some of the risks themselves and not ask their parents to take on all the risk. The children in the company took salary cuts and signed their own personal guarantees for the necessary loans to finance growth.

Expansion of the business is one approach to meeting the increased financial needs of a growing family. Three other approaches might also be considered. The first approach is to limit the number of family members who are employed and, therefore, financially dependent on the business. For example, the Hetzel family, owners of PetNet, Inc., (see Chapter 3) established employment guidelines that restricted family employment to only one spouse. This helped diversify the financial dependency of the successors' families so that some income had to be derived from outside the family business.

A second approach is to create satellite companies for family members that are vertically integrated with the core family business. For example, in one trucking business, the children own a leasing company that provides trucks and other capital equipment to the core family business. But the family business is not the only customer of the leasing company, which also provides similar services to other businesses.

For some families, this approach is accomplished by acquiring related businesses. The acquired companies are owned and operated by different branches of the family.

For family businesses with regional growth limitations, a third option should also be considered, an option that involves expanding the family business to new regions of the country. One family-owned construction company divided the United States into eight geographical regions and established branch offices in each of the regions. Each of the separate regional companies was owned by a family member, who held 51 percent of the regional business. The family holding company owned the other 49 percent.

A similar strategy has been successful for a chain of Chinese restaurants. After establishing a successful restaurant in one major metropolitan area, members of the family help another branch of the family—their brothers, sisters or cousins—open their own restaurant in a different metropolitan area, in effect creating an internal family restaurant franchise.

Of course, growth is only one option to consider. If the entrepreneurial founder and the family no longer want to take the necessary financial risks associated with growth, they may decide to position the business for sale or to just maintain the status quo. However, in both of these options, there is little future opportunity for the next generation of the family to participate in the business.

To be successful with a growth strategy, the various members of the family must be successful in their respective roles and responsibilities, and this takes management development of the future leaders of the business. That is why it is so important to establish the employment guidelines and performance criteria that were discussed in the previous chapter. The Sheridan family, anxious to implement its growth objectives, recognized the importance of the management development of family members.

The Sheridan Family
All dogs need to learn new tricks

Jerry Sheridan was a man who always believed in the importance of education. After completing his undergraduate degree in engineering, he worked for a large manufacturing company. Even after he founded his own business, Jerry returned to graduate school. There he continued his business education at the same time his new company started to grow and demand more of his time and attention. Although this was a challenge, Jerry eventually received an M.B.A. from a local university by completing its executive management program.

Jerry Sheridan's hobby of designing and hand carving ornate, ornamental candles led him to his business. While working in the engineering department of a large manufacturer, Jerry developed a patented process for manufacturing his candles. He used his engineering skills to design specialized machinery that enabled him to mass produce what had, up to then, required handcrafted expertise.

Jerry and his wife, Mary, had three children; two boys and a girl. All three developed diverse interests. Pamela, the oldest, was enrolled in an undergraduate program in architecture and planned to continue her education toward a career in urban planning. Their eldest son, Jason, was an engineer with a knack for electronic automation techniques. The youngest son, Andy, a computer expert with an undergraduate degree in computer science, had a keen ability to develop software programs and applications for industry.

After engineering school, Jason was hired on a project basis to help develop and launch a computerized system that would allow the family business to supply major national retail chains with candles for special occasions and weddings. Jason's systems automated much of the sales management needs of the company, especially the ability to interface with and supply major retailers.

Meanwhile, Andy, the second son, was also assigned on a project basis to reorganize the company's entire inventory control department, which included shipping and receiving. His proprietary software effectively computerized the entire inventory system and integrated it with those developed by his brother. He successfully reduced finished goods inventory as well as work in progress and, over the course of eight months, substantially increased overall efficiency.

These projects had relevance beyond their inherent value. The projects, and their successful completion, demonstrated to the rest of the employees that Jason and Andy were actually capable of handling a project from beginning to end. Only after both projects were successfully completed did Jerry hire them full time.

Jason was appointed manager of design and sales. But after two frustrating years, he found he did not enjoy being a manager. In addition, some of his subsequent projects turned out to be over-engineered for customer needs, ultimately cutting into company profitability. "I thought about it for a long time," Jason said. "I came to realize that I wasn't cut out for management. That realization hurt. But since I enjoyed the project work, I left management and went to work as a consultant for a larger software company."

Andy, on the other hand, enjoyed his role as manager of operations. He demonstrated that he had the ability to manage groups of people while supervising major projects. When Jerry was ready to retire, Andy took over the responsibility of leading the strategic planning meetings for the company. Through his success at leadership, it was clear that Andy would, in fact, be the family successor as president of the business.

However, before retiring, his father told Andy that he would have to earn an advanced degree if he wanted to take over leadership of the company. Jerry knew that Andy was extremely interested and excited about the opportunities in front of him, but Jerry also felt strongly that Andy needed additional education. Andy chose a local university M.B.A. program and finished his studies while working at the company part-time.

IT TAKES MORE THAN A SHEEPSKIN
TO HANDLE A HERD

While the Sheridans' case may be somewhat unusual in the commitment to advanced education, more and more successors in family business are pursuing advanced degrees, or at least formal education programs that develop their technical and managerial skills. Even when successors do not acquire advanced education, one key to success is the requirement that they remain accountable and responsible for the completion of specific projects and, ultimately, profit and loss.

As we have seen in these two family cases, the Chadwicks made a commitment to growth and the Sheridans recognized the importance of developing the management capability and expertise of the successor generation in order to preserve the long-term success of their multigenerational family businesses. These are both important, but ultimately, the success or failure of business transitions depends on the ability of the company to compete successfully in the marketplace.

In an intriguing analysis of successful family businesses and closely held companies, Hermann Simon, author of *Hidden Champions: Lessons from 500 of the World's Best Unknown Companies*[2], studied the key strategic factors that have propelled hundreds of closely held businesses to positions of world leadership.

Seventy-five percent of the businesses in his study are family-owned firms. To be included in his study, "hidden champions" must have held the number one or number two positions in their world market, had low public visibility and had annual revenues that did not exceed $1 billion. The majority of the companies were founded after World War II, with average annual revenues of approximately $130 million.

The businesses studied in Simon's book had successful business strategies, all of which were tied to becoming the niche market leader in their specific areas of expertise. These medium-sized, family-owned

---

2 Adapted and reprinted by permission of Harvard Business School Press from *Hidden Champions: Lessons from 500 of the World's Best Unknown Companies*, by Herman Simon (Boston, MA 1996), 275-276. Copyright © 1996 by the Harvard Business School Publishing Corporation. All rights reserved.

businesses grew to dominate their marketplace by implementing a common set of strategies. As Simon outlined the characteristics of these successful hidden champions, I was struck by the number of characteristics shared by my most successful clients.

To evaluate your own company, Simon suggests that you should rank both the importance of the factor and the level of performance your business has achieved for each of these nine items. With planning and focus on these key strategic factors, your family business may too become a "hidden champion:"

- Set clear, ambitious goals to be the leader in your market.
- Define your market very narrowly in order to be a niche market leader.
- Develop global orientation through worldwide sales and marketing.
- Stay close to your customers in both performance and interaction.
- Emphasize continuous innovation in products, services and processes.
- Clearly understand your competitive advantages, both in product and service.
- Know your core competencies and rely on these strengths to win in your marketplace.
- Run your company "lean and mean" and retain key employees for the long term.
- As a leader, be authoritative in your commitment to the vision and fundamentals but participative in the way you implement the strategy and details through employees.

A common thread throughout these successful hidden champions is the development of niche market strategies. Rather than trying to compete on a broad base with Fortune 500 companies, these small and medium-sized, closely held family businesses found opportunities that these larger companies could not address competitively.

The Lewis family is one example of a family that used many of these principles to grow its business through specialization in a focused marketplace.

The Lewis Family
Traveling together on the same bus

George Lewis had started a small metal fabricating shop to meet the needs of local manufacturers. It was a typical job shop that used the technical skills and craftsmanship of its labor force to make customized products in short-run quantities. It met the needs of larger manufacturers in the area. As a job shop, each project was unique, with specific design requirements, but all of the projects used the same basic skill sets, as well as machinery and equipment. Combined, these helped make his business successful. Some other job shops in the area could provide similar services, but Lewis' primary competitive advantage rested in his ability to serve his customers' needs on time and with high quality.

During the initial years of his business, Lewis' fabrication shop grew by adding customers and, accordingly, expanded the amount of equipment and square footage of the shop to meet customer demands. Growth came by increasing the number of small jobs that the shop was able to accept. The customer base expanded over the years to more than 750, of which 150 provided 80 percent of the company's revenue.

Ten years after starting the company, Lewis died unexpectedly. His two sons, Matt and Todd, had been working in the business for several years and had a strong grasp of the technical skills and, particularly, the job-estimating skills needed to continue the operation successfully.

After several years of operating the company following their father's death, Matt and Todd decided it was time to analyze the operation. As a first step, they used Pareto's Principle to study their customer list.[3] Not much had changed. Corresponding to the situation

---

3 Vilfredo Pareto, *Cours d'économie politique professé à l'Université de Lausanne.* 2 volumes. (Lausanne: Rouge. 1896-97).

during their father's leadership, 80 percent of the sales came from 20 percent of the customers.

As part of their strategic planning process, they began to study the key customers. A core group of these customers was related to the electronics business, because the Lewises had become experts at shaping and fabricating electronic equipment housings. Part of the appeal of this aspect of their business was volume. That is, while most of their job shop products were fairly short-run piecework, the equipment housing business had repeat pattern design and longer-run manufacturing.

Both of these elements made these jobs more profitable. And because of the strong relationship with the customers, the Lewis brothers decided to focus more and more of their attention on building a specialty business around this niche market.

Their traditional fabricating business had been restricted geographically to the local area, which had a large number of manufacturing companies. The Lewises supplied these companies with fabricated metal parts. However, within the local region, there were not enough electronics manufacturers to expand this portion of the business.

Consequently, the Lewises decided to initiate a market study to identify similar electronics manufacturing companies throughout the United States, and then to market their expertise to these companies. The goal was to become the premier national supplier of equipment housings to the electronics industry.

Of course, the development of this strategic objective took time. They had to gradually shift their business from a large customer base, to which they provided numerous small, unrelated projects, to a much smaller customer base, to which they sold much larger, long-production run products. The Lewis' niche market strategy eventually was successful, providing the company with several key advantages.

- ✦ They were able to diversify geographically and were no longer dependent on the economic conditions of the local market.

- ✦ By specializing in a niche market, they were able to focus their equipment purchases on specially modified machinery that gave their company a clear competitive advantage.

+ They were able to better utilize machine capacity, since they were no longer required to have enough machinery to serve a wide variety of fabricating needs. Instead, they could specially modify their equipment to the needs of key customers.

+ They were able to narrow their customer base from more than 750 customers to approximately thirty customers. And among these thirty customers, the Lewises were able to spread and distribute their sales so that no one manufacturer dominated their sales at any one time.

Finally, they no longer had to compete against a myriad of metal fabricating shops within the region. Instead, they could tailor their marketing efforts and advertising strategies to a very distinct and specialized manufacturing marketplace.

The Lewises, therefore, were able to grow their business both in size and profits by finding a unique niche market that maximized their company's core competencies and their competitive advantage. Their success depended on the combined management skills of the Lewis brothers to plan for the future, articulate a clear mission and carry out the necessary research to develop a sound business plan. With resources focused on their business, the Lewises also gained an advantage by clearly defining the priorities, roles and responsibilities of key managers—the people who would have to make the strategic plan a business reality.

The Esser Family
No sibling is an island

The Esser family recognized a similar need to clarify roles and responsibilities of family members in order to accomplish strategic objectives. The Essers' business specializes in making upscale patio and deck furniture as well as other outdoor items, such as decorative arbors. The family business also makes handcrafted water fountains for both public and private gardens. A member of the second generation of family ownership, Clint Esser is now in his seventies. He runs the company and owns half of it along with his brother, Bruce, who is three years older. Sales are about $14 million, derived largely from small, upscale boutiques on the West Coast.

Preparing for his own retirement, Clint named his son Rick, an engineer, as head of operations. Over the years, Clint had carried out both the operational needs and the sales needs of the business. As the business grew, he asked his son James to join the business as the sales manager. In a previous position, James had worked as a salesperson for a service business, which provided him with some experience in customer contact, but he had no experience in selling consumer products to retail stores.

While Clint had traditionally handled operations and sales, Clint's brother, Bruce, had handled the administration and bookkeeping responsibilities of the business. When Bruce retired and sold his share of the business to his niece and nephews, Clint recognized the need for someone to handle the financial and administrative responsibilities. Clint asked his daughter, Lisa, who had previous experience in business, to return to the family company as head of administration, human resources, and chief financial officer. At this point, Clint felt he could retire. He had three children—Rick, James and Lisa—in the company to cover the three major functional areas of responsibility—operations, sales and administration. Of course, with three family members, the company did experience pressure of sustaining growth while at the same time trying to define the diverse roles and responsibilities of all of the family members.

Two years after the children took over the company, major changes began to occur in its markets. Historically, the business had maintained itself through personal relationships, built over many years with small retail outlets. Because they had a specialty handcrafted product, the Essers sold mainly to closely held retail stores. Over the years, Esser House, Ltd. had developed long-term relationships with more than two thousand stores nationwide, most of them concentrated on the West Coast. Now, through consolidation in the industry, the small stores were going out of business and large retail chains were becoming the dominant players. Esser House, Ltd. was losing its base of business as more and more family-owned retail stores closed their doors. If it were to continue in business, the company needed a new sales strategy.

While the family members recognized that market conditions were changing through major national consolidation of the industry, they could not agree on a common approach and direction for the company. And while three successor generation family employees had titles such as vice-president of operations, vice-president of sales and vice-president of administration, there were no specific job descriptions, measurable objectives or boundaries of responsibility defining these roles. It was clear, however, that James wanted to run the company. This angered Rick, who had been working in the business for many years before James joined it. Shortly before he died, Clint decided to appoint James as company president, and gave all three of his children equal ownership in the company. However, they never met as a group to strategically plan for the future.

Growing competitive market forces, coupled with James's inadequate experience and the company's lack of planning, resulted in a dramatic drop-off in sales. In response, James implemented an aggressive sales campaign without consulting his siblings. When the campaign failed, James's brother and sister felt angry that their brother had initiated such a major move without consulting them.

EVERYONE NEEDS A PLAN

The Essers' situation clearly demonstrates that a business needs to have well-defined roles and good plans in place to meet the challenges of a changing market. Poorly defined roles leave all family members frustrated, with everyone wondering where responsibility lies. The Esser family never took the time to develop specific job descriptions, measurable objectives or areas of responsibility. They had titles, but no clear expectations that determined their success or failure.

If a business can establish specific goals and objectives connected to defined responsibilities, it is much easier to clarify the responsibilities of family members—or anyone else filling those management roles. Often family businesses will create job descriptions for each of the family members but fail to define what the exact responsibilities of the jobs are.

With a business plan in place, job descriptions defined and roles and responsibilities clarified, it becomes much easier to determine the educational and developmental needs of family members. Additionally, this scenario identifies the management and employment talent that will be required to execute a successful growth strategy.

In the case of the Essers, the family agreed that James could not make major sales decisions on his own; rather, he would talk with his siblings at regular meetings in order to make unified decisions. But with no plan and no well-defined roles, this was a family business caught in a storm of market change. Not unlike a sailboat without a rudder, one swell could upend it forever.

DEVELOPING YOUR PLAN

While some family-owned businesses start through the acquisition of an existing company, most begin through the entrepreneurial efforts of a single founder. Such entrepreneurs share common characteristics, particularly hard work, dedication and a need to control the business and all the activities within it. In the early stages of an entrepreneurial business, the founder is usually a jack of all trades. He or she must have excellent sales skills as well as technical and operational expertise; he or she may have to operate machines and buy equipment.

Many entrepreneurial companies, reflecting the diversity of the interests of the founder, mistakenly pursue too many opportunities rather than focusing on a market niche.

As successful entrepreneurial businesses grow, they are often stifled by the very strengths that made the company and its founder successful. One, in particular, is the unwillingness of the founder to narrow the focus of the business and to delegate a range of responsibilities to a management group. Working as a team, this group can grow the business successfully. Yet for most small and medium-sized businesses, the recipe for growth is the ability to develop a niche market strategy.

When explaining the strategic planning process to clients, I often use the analogy of a fishing expedition. To be successful as a fisherman, you need to first determine what kind of fish you hope to catch. When you know what you are fishing for, you can determine the type of equipment you will need, the type of bait required, the particular body of water best suited to that type of fish, and even the type of boat, electronic equipment, and time of day to fish. Furthermore, such a fishing expedition might require hiring a guide familiar with the territory.

1. Know Your Customers

The beginning of the strategic planning process, to focus the growth of your business through distinct and specific niche markets, starts with an analysis of your current business situation. To begin this process, analyze your existing customer base and the existing range of the products or services you offer. As we saw with the Lewis case, the first step was to analyze the distribution of their business among their current customers. Often, the 80/20 rule is operative. Namely, that 80 percent of the profits come from 20 percent of the customers, or 80 percent of the problems come from 20 percent of the customers. Or similarly, 80 percent of your growth potential comes from 20 percent of your current customer base. To analyze your existing business, you must have the discipline to keep accurate information about your customers as well as the categories of products or services that you offer to these customers.

In addition to understanding the demographics and characteristics of your existing customer base, it's also critical to thoroughly understand your existing product and service offerings, especially their associated profit margins. Far too few closely held family businesses have information systems that allow them to gather this information in an effective manner and establish activity-based costing. This is usually rooted in the fact that they distribute their overhead costs for general services and administration evenly across all product lines, when, in fact, some products or services are more labor-intensive than others, or require more customer service and administration activities. Another area of limited information is understanding the dynamics of your existing customer base or knowledge of your competitors. As a first step, get these issues resolved through study and analysis. Such projects provide excellent learning experiences for family successors by helping them understand the business in much greater detail.

2. Evaluate Your Strengths and Weaknesses

As a second step in the planning process, it's important to evaluate the strengths and weaknesses of your existing organization. The various strengths and weaknesses will fall into a broad range of categories, including your work force, equipment, technical skills, information systems, technology, management depth, available labor and employee morale. As part of the planning process, ask key managers and employees to critically evaluate these various components of the company in order to identify the strengths that you will be able to leverage for future growth. Also ask them to identify the weaknesses that will require focused effort for improvement. Based on this internal analysis of customers, products, services, strengths and weaknesses, you should now be in a position to more clearly define the niche market focus for your business. This focus should be the key underpinning of your core strategy or vision for the future. In a family business, this process is often complicated by its historical legacy, in particular its commitment to the vision of the founder.

For example, George Lewis had his initial success by being a diversified fabricating shop, serving a large range of customers within a regional area. Yet, in analyzing the business that their father had started, the Lewis brothers discovered that the future of the business would lie in a more focused strategy, one that addressed the needs of a special niche market on a national basis. Using a similar method, the Esser family had grown the business successfully in the past, through close personal relationships and dedicated service to a large number of small, independent retail stores. Yet changes in the marketplace and consolidation of the industry demanded that they re-evaluate this core strategy—one that had guided the goals and objectives of their business in the past. In family businesses, there is often a commitment to maintain the legacy of the past at the expense of repositioning the company to be successful in the future. Furthermore, the core competencies and strengths of the business under the successor generation may be very different from the core competencies and strengths that were characteristic of the entrepreneurial founder.

3. Determine Your Opportunities for Growth

After completing the internal analysis of the business, the next critical phase in developing a business plan is a detailed study of the marketplace, both the potential customer base and the company's competitors. To help with this process, I have found a four-quadrant grid to be a useful tool for analyzing the opportunities for the future growth of the family-owned business (see Figure 1, Strategic Marketing Matrix).

As we can see in Figure 1, the starting point is the analysis of the current customer base and current products and services offered. Strategic growth plans can move in one of two directions. As seen in the above figure, Option 1 is to continue to offer your existing products and services to new customers. This approach requires a market

		CUSTOMERS	
		Current	**New**
PRODUCTS and SERVICES	**Current**	**Current Strategy**	**Option 1** Broaden Customer Base
	New	**Option 2** Expand Products and Services	**Option 3** Develop New Businesses

Figure 1: Strategic Marketing Matrix

analysis of the potential customer base and the development of a targeted strategy to introduce your company's products or services to this new customer group. The Lewis family followed this strategy. Through their analysis of their existing customer base and product capability, they identified the opportunity to offer their manufacturing capabilities to electronic equipment manufacturing companies. The primary growth strategy involved focusing their business in this more defined niche using their core competencies. From there, they could identify and approach the specific companies likely to use their services and technical capabilities.

An alternative growth strategy, Option 2 is to expand the range of products or services that you offer to your existing customer base. In these situations, you draw upon the key characteristics of the relationship you have with your existing customers to broaden the range of products or services that they buy from your company. This requires that you do a thorough survey with your existing customer base to

95

identify why they purchase products or services from you. For example, is it quick turnaround time? Technical capability? Or is it the goodwill and trust that you've developed with the customer over the years? In addition, you need to discover from your best customers what additional items they purchase that might fit the competencies that your company can already offer, or that you could expand into by purchasing equipment that would give you that capability.

For example, the Sheridan family used this approach to grow their family-owned business. As you will recall, the Sheridans had a strong commitment to education and management development. The family had strong technical skills, with the founder being an engineer and his sons having college degrees in engineering and computer technology. In evaluating their own internal strengths, the Sheridans discovered that their technical competence and production capabilities gave them a competitive advantage in the marketplace and, therefore, provided a foundation for expanding their product offerings to existing customers.

Growth strategies that provide additional products or services to an existing customer are an example of the development of vertically integrated businesses for the family-owned company. In many family business situations, the new products and services offered to existing customers may develop within wholly-owned subsidiaries of the family business holding company. Each of the subsidiaries may be owned by the successor generation, rather than the senior generation, so that the future growth of these new business ventures accrues in the estates of the successors and, therefore, avoids being taxed in the estate of the senior generation. The strategic business plan, therefore, can be integrated with the estate planning needs of the family, in support of ownership and management succession plans. These topics will be discussed in greater detail in the next two chapters.

Entrepreneurs have the distinct capability to start new businesses. Option 3 is the most entrepreneurial strategy that could be pursued; namely, it represents the development of new products or services offered to a new customer base. Clearly, this is the most risky strategy for a business to follow, yet it is the strategy that was most successful for entrepreneurial founders. The difficulty in family-owned businesses is that the successor generation is often less entrepreneurial than the founders. However, the successors may use their skills to either promote the most successful products and services to a new customer base (Option 1) or expand the range of products and services offered to the existing customers (Option 2). In most cases, I recommend that family-owned businesses pursue either the niche market strategy taken by the Lewis family or an expanded vertical integration strategy, as seen in the Sheridan family. I do not often recommend the pursuit of the high-risk entrepreneurial strategy even though it may be at the foundation of the original family business.

The key steps in developing a strategic growth plan obviously take time, commitment and defined activities and responsibilities. Each of these steps requires considerable research and analysis before conclusions are drawn. In addition, each of these activities needs to be carried out in a team environment, so that the resources of the business are aligned with one another and focused on achieving the same goals and objectives. The lack of healthy adult communication in a family often leads to situations where there are competing agendas and the lack of a common, focused business plan for the company (see Chapter 2 for a discussion of family dynamics). The successful transition of family businesses from one generation to the next demands that the ownership group, which includes family members from the senior and successor generations, is in agreement about the strategies that will be pursued in order to develop the business in the future. The steps we have described so far will help the family agree on a common strategy.

4. Implement the Plan and Stay Focused

Once the strategy has been determined, the most critical part of the business plan must be addressed: implementation and execution. I have worked with many closely held businesses where the planning process has taken place, yet the day-to-day operations of the business have been unaffected by these specific strategic goals and objectives. In particular, the momentum of the past, the "way we've done business," affects all the day-to-day actions and activities of the company and may impede implementation of the new strategic goals and objectives. For example, the Lewis' strategy was to develop a nationally based niche business in the electronic housing industry. This strategy required not only that they pursue new customers in the electronics industry, but also that they have the discipline to say no to some of their existing customers. These were customers that no longer met the company's criteria for customers that would support its strategic goals and objectives. Perhaps this is one of the most difficult aspects of implementing and executing a strategic plan—staying committed and focused to the criteria that will shape the future goals and objectives of the business.

Another issue that frequently undermines the strategic planning process in closely held companies is having new opportunities appear on the horizon that were not anticipated through the strategic planning process. These new opportunities frequently fall into the entrepreneurial category (Option 3); that is, they are opportunities that neither come from an existing customer nor are shaped by the niche market strategy that has been determined through the strategic planning process. Certainly, any new opportunity needs to be evaluated, since it might just hold the key to the future of the business. However, family-owned businesses often fail to step back and complete a strategic analysis of the new opportunity and, furthermore, fail to modify their existing strategic commitments if they, in fact, decide that they will take on this new business venture.

So far, I've described some of the basic steps that family-owned businesses should follow in order to articulate the strategic business plan. The actual execution of the plan requires clear goals and objectives, with defined responsibilities and measurable criteria for carrying out the actions necessary to implement the plan. Once the basic structure of the strategic plan has been determined, it is critically important to develop specific actions to implement the plan.

In family businesses, this often provides an opportunity for members of the successor group to be given key strategic responsibilities, not only to carry out their existing job responsibilities but also to carry through and be team leaders of specific goals and objectives. For example, the Lewis family's plan required an analysis of the market opportunities by identifying other electronics companies that could become customers. Part of the strategic plan involved overseeing a marketing analysis, in particular, identifying and evaluating future customers. This aspect of the plan was delegated to one of the Lewis brothers, although it clearly was beyond the scope of his existing job description. As a group, the managers of the company established specific targeted dates for the completion of the market analysis, and one of the brothers was held accountable for meeting these targeted responsibilities.

5. Hold Regular Strategic Review Meetings

Besides defining specific responsibilities in order to implement a new business strategy, family businesses must make a commitment to hold regular strategic review sessions. These are to make sure that the plan is carried out and is on target. I've discovered, in my many years facilitating strategic planning sessions of closely held companies, that there is a natural tendency to become focused on the day-to-day responsibilities of responding to customer demands and to lose sight of the implementation of the strategic goals of the business. Therefore, I have come to believe that it is critically important for family-owned businesses to make a commitment to hold, at a minimum, quarterly meetings to review the strategic plan. During these review meetings, only long-range strategic issues may be addressed. No day-to-day operational issues should consume the meeting time.

6. Define Clear Roles and Responsibilities

By establishing specific goals and objectives, which have defined responsibilities attached to them, it is much easier to clarify the roles and duties of family members, and to establish accountability standards. Such standards not only guide the implementation process, they also support development of family members as future leaders of the business. Family businesses often create job descriptions for each of the family members, but they fail to put any "meat on the bones" of these descriptions. That is, they fail to define, in measurable terms, what the success or failure is within any specific job.

In my judgment, family businesses need to have two major components within the job description of each family member as well as within that of nonfamily managers. The first component concerns the day-to-day responsibilities and expectations for the specific job. For example, if a family member is the vice-president of operations, with day-to-day responsibility for overseeing the scheduling and production requirements of the business, what kind of expectations should be established in areas such as employee retention, waste and on-time delivery? All of these, and similar items, can be quantified, and family members can be held accountable for meeting these standards. The second component of the roles and responsibilities for family members and other managers involves their responsibilities regarding strategic goals and objectives. Again, these strategic goals and objectives need to be clearly defined, with measurable standards and dates for accomplishment.

With a business plan in place, job descriptions defined, and roles and responsibilities for meeting strategic objectives clarified, it then becomes much easier to determine the educational and developmental needs of family members. It is then also easier to identify the additional management and employee talent required to carry out a successful growth strategy through the strategic plan.

Questions to Discuss About Business Planning:

The strategic business plan determines the best structure for the organization of a company to achieve its goals. Implementation of the plan requires that managers and other employees have defined roles and responsibilities with measurable performance standards. Families in business should integrate their strategic business plan with the long-term goals and objectives of the family. To start this integration process, respond to these questions:

+ Does each family employee have clearly defined roles and responsibilities in the business? Explain.

+ Have nepotistic practices been identified and eliminated so that the business attracts and retains the most competent managers?

+ Does your company have a strategic business plan? Have all generations and shareholders been involved in the plan?

+ Has your company devised a plan to accommodate its growth? What positions might you have to add or remove to develop an infrastructure to support the growth?

+ When was the last time you studied your marketplace? How would you best use your family and nonfamily members to create a new marketing strategy?

+ The Family Business Assessment Tool™ measures three success factors concerning business planning: Business structure, nonfamily management and business strategy. How would you rank your business on these factors?

PASSING
THE BATON

Chapter 5

A recent national survey reported that 42.7 percent of all family business owners intend to retire in the next five years.[1] With life expectancy now approaching the mid-eighties, statistics reveal that the real challenge for family businesses is not ownership transition at death, but rather management succession before the senior generation retires. The elder generation should not wait to ponder the next step for the business. Conversely, the successor generation should take responsibility and play a key role in establishing the new order. The truth is, the responsibility for successful management transitions rests with both generations.

---

1 Arthur Anderson/MassMutual, *American Family Business Survey* (Springfield, MA: MassMutual, 1997),

To better understand the continuity factors that are critical for family-owned businesses, our firm has conducted research with family businesses throughout the United States, England, Scotland, Ireland and Australia, using The Family Business Assessment Tool™ 2. Of the over five hundred participants in the survey, approximately half were from the senior generation, while the other half were from the successor generation. The results of the research provide a very broad spectrum of perspectives on the issues facing family businesses. However, one central fact emerges—the respondents emphasized that management transition, not estate transfer, is the most important continuity factor that must be resolved. When we analyzed the divergent responses on the survey, we were able to pinpoint key issues that need to be addressed for the successful continuity of family business from one generation of management to the next.

- ✦ First, the retiring owners need to establish long-term personal financial security, as well as protection of their health insurance needs.

- ✦ Second, the retiring presidents or family managers must be willing to let go of their current roles and responsibilities and empower the new management team to make its own critical business decisions.

- ✦ Third, the successor generation must be experienced and qualified, with a demonstrated ability to manage the business successfully for the future.

Obviously, smooth transitions within the management responsibilities of a family-owned business are more successful if the underlying groundwork has been completed. This groundwork, which has been described in the previous chapters, includes the development of effective communications and adult relationships among the family members, clear employment criteria and performance requirements to

---

2 Dean R. Fowler and James Bashford, "Love, Power, and Money: Implications of International Research with Family Businesses for Collaborative Consulting," in *Proceedings of the 1999 Family Firm Institute Conference* (Boston: The Family Firm Institute, 2000), 126-135.

measure the competency and capability of the successors. Finally, the business needs a clearly articulated strategic business plan for long-term financial success.

Please remember that the retirement and management transition planning process is much more effective if the proper financial planning has been completed. In this way, the senior generation is no longer dependent upon the long-term success of the business and can objectively help to implement the plan without focusing on their personal financial needs. The following case studies demonstrate how several families addressed these issues.

The Shoberg Family
Handing down a business first—and a legacy second

After serving in the Korean War, Jeff Shoberg returned to his hometown in Wisconsin, ready to take on the challenges of a new career. Prior to the war, Jeff had worked in a business owned by the family of his wife, Kay. As the son-in-law, he had always hoped to move on and build his own business, separate and independent from his in-laws. An opportunity to sell plastic injection molded products became available, and with the financial support of Kay's family, Jeff was able to launch a new business.

Jeff was the consummate salesman, successfully building the foundation of his business around strong customer service. Over the years, Shoberg Plastics grew substantially, and during the mid-1980s, both of his sons became involved in the company. The older son, Robert, helped his father with key customer accounts and gradually took over more and more of the responsibilities of the sales function. Jeff's younger son, Andy, had strong technical skills, after earning an undergraduate degree in manufacturing engineering.

Typical of most closely held business owners, Jeff Shoberg's business represented the majority of his total net worth—in his case approximately 85 percent of his total net worth. Jeff recognized that he should diversify his financial holdings and establish a strong financial base for his future income needs. Jeff and his wife had always dreamed of owning a year-round home on one of Wisconsin's beautiful lakes. With two capable sons in the business, who were becoming increasingly experienced in both sales and operations, Jeff recognized that he could begin planning for his retirement.

As part of his planning, Jeff took several critical steps. Working with a financial planner, he designed a qualified retirement plan for the corporation. He also drew a large enough salary to start diversifying his financial holdings by growing his personal stock portfolio. As the business grew and additional building space was required, the Shobergs decided to own the buildings independent of the corporation. They entered into long-term lease agreements with the company to generate rental income. By the time Jeff reached his sixtieth birthday, he was no longer financially dependent on the business, thanks to his financial planning. And while it was still important that the business continue to be financially successful in order to finance their lease payments, Jeff and Kay Shoberg knew that they would be able to live a comfortable lifestyle independent of the long-term success of their family-owned company.

"I also wanted to free my children from having to feel they had to run the business for our benefit after we retired," Jeff Shoberg said. "They needed to be able to make good business decisions, independent of our needs."

While Jeff Shoberg took the initiative to develop a diversified financial portfolio and to plan for the long-term financial needs of his retirement years, too many family business owners fail to develop financial security separate and independent from their closely held business. Rather than diversifying their assets, many family business owners are totally dependent on the long-term financial success of the business to generate their retirement income. In fact, in many cases, the primary retirement plan of the senior generation rests on their children—the children who will operate the company in order to generate enough cash to finance their parents' retirement years.

These retirement planning issues are equally complex when a family-owned business is moving from the second to third generation, and has a group of siblings or cousins who are all owners of the business. This was the case with the Arnold family.

The Arnold Family
It takes work to make the scales balance

Three Arnold brothers own and operate a commercial fishing business in Maine called Arnold Fishing, Ltd. The company was founded by their father, Lou Arnold, when the oldest son, Hal, was sixteen. Hal has worked at the company since its beginning. His two brothers, Lee and Jack, entered the business approximately ten years later. The Arnold brothers, now in their fifties and sixties, own equal shares of the company. Hal indicated that he would like to retire at age sixty-two. Because Hal had no children interested in working at the family business, he told his brothers that at his retirement, he would like to sell his stock and cash out.

During their careers, the Arnold brothers divided their responsibilities. Hal was in charge of the fishing operations. Lee was in charge of sales and marketing and Jack handled the administration, which included finance, accounting and office management.

With this division of responsibilities and their equal ownership, the brothers agreed to have equal compensation. As an S-Corporation, they also shared the profits of the business on an equal basis. Over the years, there were very few disagreements among the brothers, mainly because they had clearly defined their roles and responsibilities. The business had been very successful, growing at a rate of approximately 10 percent a year.

However, as Hal approached retirement age, the brothers could not agree on Hal's retirement exit strategy. While equality had been their norm for the past twenty years, Hal felt strongly that his retirement plan should recognize the length of service that he had committed to the business. As the brother who had worked in the firm longer than his younger brothers, he felt strongly that he should be rewarded accordingly.

Approximately ten years ago, as part of their estate planning process, Hal, Lee and Jack had entered into a buy-sell agreement. This buy-sell agreement had been designed primarily to deal with federal estate tax issues, not with retirement issues. One provision of the buy-sell agreement included a discount on the value of minority shares for federal estate tax planning purposes. Hal, as the oldest of the brothers, was concerned that this discount would also apply to the sale of his stock for retirement purposes. He felt it was inherently unfair that, after working longer in the business than his brothers, he would receive 25 percent less for his stock (if sold back to his brothers or the corporation at his retirement) than he would receive if the whole company were sold upon his retirement. Why should he have to give up substantial value of his ownership position just because he was the oldest and wanted to retire before his brothers? Based on the history of equality of ownership and compensation, Hal, Lee and Jack agreed that they should find an alternative solution to meet the retirement needs of Hal and also address the long-term retirement needs of all three of the brothers.

The situation facing the Arnold family poses a common issue—how do you achieve financial fairness? How do you treat fairly a minority shareholder who decides to retire before the business is sold? How could Hal get enough money to continue to enjoy his lifestyle and still accomplish the long-term estate planning goals necessary to deal with the federal government? And finally, how can these financial issues be addressed without jeopardizing the ability of the business to function and have adequate capital to reinvest in future growth?

From Hal's perspective, the simplest solution was to sell the business. Because he had no children who were interested in future employment at the company, Hal had no long-term commitment to the corporation. A sale of the business would allow Hal to maximize his ownership interest, and then to take the proceeds from the sale of the business and invest these in a diversified stock portfolio. The valuation expert hired by the company determined that the business' true market value was approximately $24 million. Hal knew that with $8 million to invest, he would be financially secure for the remainder of his life. His brothers, however, still had ten years to work in the business, and felt that the best way to maximize their long-term financial success was to continue their involvement with the business and manage its growth successfully into the future. In addition, Jack had two sons who were pursuing college degrees directly related to commercial fishing and they intended to come to work at the family-owned business.

In order to resolve this retirement issue, the Arnold brothers agreed to revise their buy-sell agreement to include provisions for retirement planning. After much discussion and negotiation with their legal and financial advisors, Hal, Lee and Jack Arnold agreed that retiring owners could receive full value for their stock ownership if they were willing to accept a fifteen-year payout for the value of the stock. On the other hand, if the retiring brother wanted to receive a lump sum payment, they would use a 10 percent minority discounting provision to offset the cost of a loan.

The company also had established a qualified 401(k) retirement plan. The brothers agreed to start funding a nonqualified retirement program that was designed to equalize the benefits that each brother would receive upon retirement. Since Hal was retiring first, his nonqualified retirement plan would be funded more quickly than that of his brothers. With these provisions in place, the conflict over the retirement plan was resolved, and clear and defined procedures were in place to handle the retirement of each of the Arnold brothers.

FINANCIAL PLANNING STRATEGIES

When no longer employed in the business after retirement, many of the financial advantages of employment-related income and perks are no longer available to the closely held business owner. As we saw with both the Shoberg family and the Arnolds, retirement planning is a very complex financial process that must address the long-term financial needs of both the retiring owner and of the business.

For the owners, these issues are often entwined in their individual estate planning objectives. In general, I believe that the owners of closely held companies should start planning for their long-term financial needs at least fifteen years before they reach retirement age. The goal should be to become as financially independent of the business as possible, so that the long-term success or failure of the family-owned business will not impact the financial security of the retired family members.

In working with qualified financial planning experts, both generations should explore several issues:

1. Retirement Plans

Establish a federally qualified retirement plan for your company. These plans allow income to be invested in the retirement planning vehicle on a pre-tax basis. In addition, the assets within the retirement plan grow on a tax-free basis until they are withdrawn. With certain exceptions, IRS rules require that such federally qualified plans have penalties for early withdrawal prior to age 59½ and also require that withdrawals begin by age 70½.

2. Nonqualified Plans

Explore nonqualified retirement plans for yourself and your key managers, because they offer a favorable way to set aside money for the retirement needs of both the senior and successor generations. Nonqualified plans are most often used for owners and other key employees, including family successors, who have already fully funded a qualified plan. They also are used to provide selective benefits that are not offered to all employees.

3. Deferred Compensation Agreements

Deferred compensation agreements are a method to provide income during retirement to compensate a key employee for past services. It is recognized that the owners of closely held companies often work for less income than comparable job positions would require. This income can be deferred for future years to augment a retirement income.

4. Real Estate and Equipment Ownership

Like Jeff Shoberg, many owners of closely held businesses own the land and buildings used by the business, and sometimes certain equipment, separate from the corporation itself. This strategy has two distinct advantages. First of all, it allows for a stream of rental income that is independent of employment in the family business. In addition, as the value of the property grows over the years, the owners' net worth is diversified outside the operating business. And if the business fails, is sold or outgrows the existing buildings, these properties can be valuable assets to the owners of the business.

5. Buy-Sell Agreements

As with the Arnold brothers, many buy-sell agreements are written for estate planning transfer reasons but fail to address the need of retiring owners from the business. In multiple owner situations, where groups of minority shareholders work in the company, it is critical that the family address the methods and procedures that will be used to handle the repurchase of stock of retiring shareholders. Certainly, the stock buyout provision between the successor and senior generations is also a key strategy for successful management transitions in family business. To the degree that a retired shareholder continues to have financial interest in the business, it will become much more difficult for the retired shareholder to let go of his or her roles and responsibilities in the business. Finally, buy-sell agreements should define how stock will be valued and purchased by the corporation or other stockholders in case of death, disability, termination or divorce.

6. Grantor-Retained Annuity Trusts (GRAT)

Another vehicle that should be explored for retirement transitions includes the use of a grantor-retained annuity trust, better known as a GRAT. A GRAT provides an opportunity to transfer stock to the successors while generating income to the shareholder who establishes the GRAT. Basically, a shareholder places stock in this trust but retains an annuity income interest in the trust. The trust then pays an annual sum of annuity payments to the shareholder, and at the end of the term of the trust, the stock transfers to the beneficiaries of the trust. GRATs, therefore, serve the dual purpose of transferring stock, often at a discounted value, to the successor generation owners of the company while generating income to the existing owners of the company.

These and other financial planning tools are critical for the successful management transition in a closely held business. On the one hand, to the degree that closely held business owners maintain their ownership positions in the company, they will continue to have a strong vested interest in asserting management control over key corporate decisions and the investment of business capital. On the other hand, to the degree that business owners are financially independent of the family-owned business, it is much easier for them to let go of management responsibilities and remove themselves from decision making in the company.

LETTING GO CAN TAKE SOME TIME

Letting go of the control of a closely held business is much easier when the financial issues have been addressed and adequately resolved. But, in addition to the issues of money, the non-financial issues associated with power also complicate successful management transitions in closely held companies. Differences in leadership style and the importance of the allegiance of management staff to the senior executives are crucial elements determining successful management transitions. This was certainly the case with the Angi family.

The Angi Family
One leader, one spotlight

The Angi Corporation is a general contracting business located in a rural part of Iowa. Doug Angi ran the business throughout his life, developing a good reputation as a contractor as well as a respected land developer. Doug had five children, three of whom entered the business after completing college and worked full time. His daughter Jessica, who decided to focus her attention on her family, worked part-time at the business, enjoying the flexibility provided through her employment in the family company. Doug's eldest son, Jim, entered the business after receiving a masters' degree in finance, having worked for several years for one of the larger national accounting firms.

Jim clearly had the strongest academic expertise, as well as outside business experience. However, stylistically, Jim was very different from his father, and often Jim and Doug had disagreements over the appropriate way to make key business decisions. Ron, the second eldest son, ran the construction side of the business. He had long-term experience working as a journeyman carpenter and was deeply respected by the work force. Ted, who was the youngest of the three sons, worked closely with his father in the real estate development side of the business, attending regular meetings with his father. Ted, through the years of work with his father, got to know the key people in the community and local governments who were critical to the successful development of real estate projects.

Over the years, as Doug Angi's business grew, he came to depend on a strong support staff. This was a group of nonfamily employees who carried out the day-to-day operations of the business, based on decisions and strategies that Doug had chosen to pursue. While Jim, the eldest son, was always considered to be in line to succeed his father, there was often ongoing tension between father and son, particularly Jim's reluctance to work with Doug's key support staff. Like his father, Jim was affable and worked well with clients, but he also wanted to have more control over the business, which did not sit well with Doug, who was still several years away from retirement. In addition, Doug favored most of the decisions from his support group, but Jim rarely agreed with them. What Jim wanted was to develop his own staff and he wanted to promote new people into important positions within the company.

These tensions over leadership and management style between Doug and Jim are common in family businesses. Often the founding entrepreneur has developed a strong support staff that carries out his or her wishes and desires as dutiful lieutenants. This was the case with Doug, who had a very strong control and command style of leadership. Doug made all the decisions, followed through on the details and depended on the support staff to carry out his wishes. Jim, on the other hand, preferred a team perspective and a participative approach. He wanted people who could make their own decisions, take increased responsibility and coordinate their efforts through strategic planning activities. He was frustrated with his father's people, primarily because of their inability to make their own decisions and their reluctance to be held accountable for implementing their own strategies.

Of course, Doug's people were loyal to him and not to Jim. Because of Doug's confidence in his circle of key people, he believed that the company would suffer if he began spending more time in retirement and lost his support staff. Because of the differences in leadership style and the increasing tensions between Jim and Doug, many of Doug's loyal staff indicated that they would leave the business if Jim were given more responsibilities. Therefore, from Doug's perspective, while Jim had the academic and business experience to make important decisions, Doug did not feel that Jim could manage the business and provide the necessary leadership. In fact, what Doug really wanted was for Jim to become part of his regular support staff and carry out Doug's directives and strategic objectives while he spent more time at his Florida home.

Jim, on the other hand, felt that his father was simply not letting go of the business. While Doug frequently stated that he was retiring, he continued to maintain regular and daily contact with the company and with his support staff. The tensions between Jim and his father were mounting, and the conflict started to affect Doug's support team.

This situation between Doug and his son Jim, was complicated by two key issues. The first was Doug's financial situation. Doug still owned the business and he depended on the success of the business for his own personal income needs. In addition, as the owner of a real estate development and construction company, Doug was still personally liable for the outstanding debt to the financial community. It was clear, as I worked with this father and son, that Doug's need to maintain his control over the business could not be resolved until he no longer had the financial liabilities of the business through his personal guarantees and had achieved financial independence separate from the business.

In addition to these financial issues was an even greater disagreement between father and son over management style. Doug had always been a hands-on manager. Jim, on the other hand, wanted to delegate responsibilities to the rest of the management team. In addition, Doug and Jim argued over long-term company strategy. Doug, who had built the business through high financial risk, now wanted to lessen his financial exposure. Thus, Doug was more interested in managing existing properties and completing existing construction projects. Jim, on the other hand, saw the company's long-term future in higher-risk real estate development opportunities. Jim complained about his father watching over his shoulder all the time and Doug was frustrated with Jim pushing for change, as well as Jim's desire to take on more debt through the business. Doug felt that his son was trying to push him out of the company. Unfortunately, this is a classic struggle faced by many family businesses: The two generations are trapped in their own perspectives of the same issues. But the issues don't end here.

While the struggle over leadership presents itself as a form of inter-personal conflict between the two generations, the real source of the problem, as we've seen with Doug and Jim, is with each individual's personal conflict with their own needs. For example, Doug had three personal needs that were inconsistent with one another. He had a need to enjoy retirement, a need to pass the business on to the future gener-ation and a need to protect his financial concerns and key employees who had worked with him through the years. How could Doug let go of the business so that it would succeed in the future, yet continue to control the business in order to protect his own interests?

Doug's son, Jim, also had competing needs. On the one hand, Jim wanted to control his own destiny and build a business to protect his future. On the other hand, he had a strong loyalty to and respect for his father and his family in general. How could Jim manage his father's business, protect his parents' needs and interests, as well as those of his siblings, and at the same time, honor his own need to be in charge of his own destiny? Doug and Jim were trying to share the same spot-light. They were both trying to lead the company and call the shots, all at a time when the actual transfer of the company and control of the operation had not been worked out.

As we saw in Chapter 4 on strategic business planning, it is critical for a family-owned business to reach common agreement on business tactics and objectives. But whose long-term strategy should get most consideration? Typically in the transfer between the senior and suc-cessor generation, the senior generation is more likely to give greater weight to financial security than the successor generation. The senior generation wants to protect the assets that it has grown, while the suc-cessor generation is willing to take risks to continue building the business for the future. However, without agreement over a core strategy, there will be ongoing conflict between the two generations, particularly as each becomes increasingly frustrated with the risks that the other does or does not want to take.

For the Angi Corporation, these issues were clear. Either Jim had to accept that he was, in fact, managing his father's business for his father's benefit, and that as president, he was little more than a part of his father's team, or Jim had to be willing to take on more personal financial risk for the business. Jim had to develop a business strategy that would remove financial risk from his father.

In addition, Doug and Jim had to recognize the differences that they had in their management and leadership styles. This issue had a significant impact on the executive staff that Doug had developed over the years. Because Doug used a command and control approach, his most trusted key employees were those who implemented, rather than those who acted with initiative. Jim, on the other hand, wanted to use a team approach to the development of his management group. Jim needed key people who were competent team players and took responsibility for growing and managing aspects of the business that were under their individual control. The result was that from Doug's perspective, the key executives who had been faithful and loyal to him over the years were the best people for the future of the business. They were people he felt needed to be protected. But in Jim's view, his father's key people lacked the capability to be strong leaders and carry the company forward.

THE CAPTAIN NEEDS TO STEER THE SHIP

Conflicts over leadership are common in family businesses, especially as successors reach their middle thirties. This coincides with the time when most senior generation owners are nearing retirement and considering the options of spending less time and energy focused on the day-to-day activities of their company. The conflict between the two generations as they struggle to share the spotlight is a symptom of their inability to clarify their own personal needs, agree on business objectives, set clear boundaries of responsibility and articulate performance expectations. To resolve conflicts over leadership, the senior and successor generations must be able to discuss these critical issues honestly and objectively, and find a middle ground that meets their competing needs.

Ultimately, the issue is one of control. Who has the final word? Is the successor's role primarily to manage a parent's business according to their parent's terms or is it to develop and design their own business strategy to take the family legacy in a new direction? The issues of control must be resolved. Ultimately these become the critical issues in the ownership transition of the business, which will be discussed in more depth in the next chapter.

After considerable discussion of these issues, Doug and Jim Angi found a solution. Doug agreed to reduce his personal financial risk in the business by selling some of the partnership real estate investments he had created over the years. Jim would spearhead all new developments and take on new investment partners. Eventually he would assume all the financial liability and Doug would no longer be bound by any personal guarantees. He and Jim agreed to structure an owner-financed buyout of the family business. All of the stock in the operating company gradually transferred to Jim.

As the Angi Corporation case demonstrated, successful management transitions ultimately depend on the willingness of the senior generation to let go.

Successful transitions also depend on the capability and the competency of the successors. The new generation must be willing to take on some financial risk in order to go forward.

In fact, the key question that all business owners must resolve is whether they have family members who have the qualifications and capabilities to responsibly manage the company and carry it forward.

Competent successors will manage the business successfully and reduce the financial risk the family and the retiring senior generation needs to face. But if the successor generation lacks good business skills and experience, it could jeopardize the future of the company.

118

Incompetent successors, in turn, require the continued involvement and interjection of the senior generation in business decisions.

Our next case, the Argyll family, shows how the issue of competency may be addressed by using an outside board of directors and formal assessments to determine the qualifications of family members for future leadership in the company.

The Argyll Family
You need a ticket if you want to play

Gordon Argyll owned a waterproofing and drywall business that specialized in commercial construction. He had three sons, none of whom worked in the company. However, the oldest son, Nate, had worked for another construction company for the past ten years, where he had demonstrated his management and business skills and was promoted to vice-president of operations. The family had established guidelines and criteria requiring outside employment as a condition for work in the family business (see Chapter 3).

Nate was planning his career so that he would be qualified to return to the family business. Argyll Waterproofing, Inc. owned by Gordon Argyll, had grown through the years under his leadership. As Gordon reached his late fifties, he decided to turn over more of the day-to-day responsibilities of operating the company to a nonfamily president, Tim Harris. Harris had been recruited from outside the company because of his strong experience in the construction industry. Even though he was not a family member, Tim worked exceptionally well in the company, and in the next three years he grew the business beyond Gordon's expectations.

However, after three-and-a-half years in the job, Harris was diagnosed with a rare form of cancer and was told by his doctors that his prognosis would be better if he retired and focused on his treatment. These unfortunate circumstances created the opportunity for Gordon's son, Nate, to return to the family business. As a vice-president in another construction company which also was family-owned, Nate recognized that he would never progress to the top position in that company. His best opportunity to run a company lay with Argyll Waterproofing. Nate contacted his father and indicated his interest in the vacated president's position.

"It was a tough time," Nate recalled. "Tim was also a family friend, and he'd done so much for the company. I didn't want to appear opportunistic, but at the same time, I felt I could really help. I felt I was ready."

Gordon Argyll agreed, but he had wisely set up an independent decision making process. Gordon had established a strong outside board of directors and had used the board both for the hiring of Tim Harris as well as for a professional overview of the strategic and financial needs of the business. Gordon explained to Nate that the hiring decision would rest in the hands of the board, which had the responsibility for screening candidates and making the final selection.

Clearly, from Gordon Argyll's perspective, if a family member were qualified, then the family member would receive preference over non-family candidates. The family member would have to demonstrate, however, that he or she was as good or better than any of the other candidates under consideration.

Gordon felt this requirement was critical to the long-term protection of the company, which was an asset that benefited the entire family. Gordon did not want to jeopardize the company just to maintain family leadership. Nate Argyll was required to submit to the normal screening procedures and selection process for the hiring of key executives at Argyll Waterproofing, Inc.

Since the Argyll board controlled the selection process, it set three criteria for the hiring process. First, it required personality testing and assessments. These were meant to identify the strengths and weaknesses of Nate's personal style and leadership potential.

Nate completed several assessment questionnaires and also went through an interviewing process with the industrial psychology firm that had been used by the company over the years to evaluate potential new candidates and to review key personnel for promotions. The assessment process concluded that Nate was extremely qualified and capable of taking on a critical leadership role at the company.

Second, the board insisted that any candidate for the post had experience in a related industry. Nate clearly met this criterion, having risen to the vice-president of operations post at a construction company. Finally, the board had a strong commitment to Tim Harris, who would maintain his employment in the company for as long as he chose. Therefore, it was critical that the candidate was willing to work out a transition process with Tim Harris.

Although Nate had operations and management experience at the construction company, he understandably lacked a strong knowledge of Argyll's existing customer base—a critical issue to the board and to the future of the company. To ease the transition and to prepare Nate for the president's role, the board agreed to hire him for the post of executive vice-president. But with the hiring came the understanding that Nate would become involved in the customer service, customer relations and estimating procedures of the company before he could move to the presidency.

Because of Gordon Argyll's commitment to strong business principles, including an outside board and criteria for the hiring of family members, Argyll made a successful transition at a difficult time in the company's development. Clearly the selection of competent successors is the most pivotal decision that an entrepreneur needs to make. In my judgment, the presidential succession process actually begins when the family determines the rules for employing family members (see Chapter 3). If no rules of entry have been defined and no performance standards enforced, there is less likelihood that the next leader of the family business will successfully guide the company in the future. For the Argylls, the decision to require outside employment and demonstrated work experience was critical to resolving the management transition issues.

SUCCESSOR INITIATIVE—WHAT IT TAKES

In addition to having criteria in place and procedures for the selection of key family members to executive positions, the other critical dimension in successful family business transitions involves the initiative taken by the successors themselves. This is often an overlooked aspect of successful management transitions.

Since 1983, I have led roundtable peer groups for successors in family-owned businesses. The members of these groups come from successful family businesses that are committed to developing the future managers and leaders of their family corporations. Through my experience with these successful family businesses, three critical characteristics have emerged that define successful management transitions, particularly the transition of the presidency of a family-owned business:

+ First, successful transitions depend on the successor being involved and taking initiative in the transition process itself.
+ Second, successful transitions require a strong management team in place, one that can work effectively with the successor.
+ Third, successful transitions recognize the need for meaningful retirement opportunities and activities for the senior generation.

Too many successors complain that their parent or parents will not let go. Feeling they lack the power to deal with business issues, these successors whine about the problems of the business, placing blame on their parents. In contrast, next-generation leaders who have been successful in making the transition to the presidency know that the most important element in their success was their willingness to be proactive, rather than reactive, in their approach to succession. The successor needs to be comfortable with developing his or her own game plan and alternative approaches to issues and problems. The proactive approach enables family members to be confident that the successor has the leadership and management ability to find solutions, rather than just complain about problems.

The Helms Family
Controlling your own destiny

For many years, Kenneth Helms, the founder of Specialty Plastics Corporation, hoped that one of his two children would emerge as the next leader of the firm. The company had enjoyed several years of steady success. A maker of high-end plastic components for the medical market, Specialty Plastics was known for its product quality and exceptional customer service.

Eager to determine which sibling would be the next president, Kenneth gave each of his children, his daughter, Jean, and son, Mark, projects to accomplish in the area of market expansion. Jean and Mark gladly accepted the challenge and both worked diligently to complete their assignments.

However, during the course of their work, Jean and Mark felt increased competitive tension to be the first one to successfully complete their respective projects. Each recognized that the first one to finish would have the best shot at becoming the successor to their father. While Kenneth's intentions were good, the plan didn't generate the "creative tension" he had planned. Jean and Mark, realizing what their father had done, became increasingly dissatisfied with the situation. As an alternative, they took the situation into their own hands and met together, independent of their father.

"We realized what our dad was trying to accomplish," Mark said. "But we felt there were better ways to get there."

"Mark and I have worked together in one way or another for years," Jean added. "We know and, probably most importantly, agree upon, each of our strengths and weaknesses. Working as a team, we're in the best position to take the business forward."

They designed a transition plan that made sense for them, drawing on their individual strengths as well as personal goals and objectives. But they also took into account their father's needs.

Mark and Jean focused on developing specific roles and responsibilities that would best meet the needs of the corporation. At the same time, they recognized the need to maintain the company's outstanding reputation for quality and customer service. After they created an organized transition plan, each of the children took additional initiatives. They entered educational programs to broaden their knowledge base and to achieve specific roles that they had carved out for themselves. Jean participated in my Forum for Family Business, and Mark entered a master's of business administration program at a local university. Next, they presented their transition plan to their father and asked for his support. Mark and Jean were able to take charge of the management transition themselves, coordinating the steps they needed for success.

"I was extremely proud of what they did," their father said. "Not only did they take the initiative, they took the *right* initiatives. I felt comfortable turning over more of the operation to them so that I could work on other issues."

As we saw in the situation between Doug and Jim Angi, the leadership style and management development needs of the corporation are also critical to successful management transitions. Many successful business founders are both entrepreneurial and autocratic. This was certainly the case with Doug. He had grown his business through long hours, a passion for excellence and hands-on control of all aspects of the business. His entrepreneurial style was particularly successful during the early development and growth of the business. However, the founder's management style often becomes a roadblock to the success of the management transition. As a business reaches maturity, growing in employment and managerial complexity, a professional management team is often necessary to lead it into the future.

For successors, the transition to leadership entails much more than taking over the roles that their parents had filled. The successors often must redefine themselves, taking the initiative either to develop their own executive staff or to transform the existing management team. Furthermore, to take over as president, a successor must find a competent manager to fill his or her current position. One of my clients likes to call this "backfill." Before he can assume the increased responsibility of taking over the presidency, he must first "backfill" his current position, developing his own successor. At this stage in the life of the business, when management transition and retirement are critical, clear communication, teamwork and business planning become most important for the continuity of the business.

OPEN YOUR PARACHUTE

Family businesses that successfully transition from one generation to the next have made a series of commitments on many levels. They commit to:

+ Meeting the needs of both the current and future owners.
+ Managing the company to the best of their ability.
+ Fostering a management team that is responsive to the new leadership of the business.

This may require them to step out of familial roles and become objective participants in running a successful company. If sons or daughters feel that they can never challenge their parents' way of thinking, the company could suffer, both during and after a succession period. Conversely, the senior generation needs to take an honest, objective look at their children in the business and make some difficult decisions about what is best for the company, not the family.

A successful succession plan must also balance the financial needs of the business with the long-term security needs of the retiring generation. The senior members of the business cannot let go of their management role if they are financially tied to the company for regular income. Their financial needs are also changing, and with that in mind, they will make decisions based on personal security rather than the long-range view of what is best for the company. Successors, on the other hand, are not thinking so much about the present as they are about the future. They are eager to take the company forward. This situation can spell disaster for the company when the two generations focus on differing goals and needs.

As we have seen through the examples of families in this chapter, successful management transitions require considerable planning; both financially, for the retirement needs of the owners, and structurally, for the needs of the business. Retirement planning issues are also coupled with the estate planning issues, the topic of the next chapter.

Questions to Discuss About Management Succession Planning:

The transition to new leadership is a double-edged sword. On the one hand, the senior generation must be willing to let go and pass the baton to the next generation. On the other hand, the successor generation must demonstrate both the maturity and competency to take over the reins of the business. Management transitions are complex and require formalization of the process for the transition of the business. Discuss the following topics to develop a management succession process for your business:

- ✦ Do you have a written management succession plan in place that deals with the future management and continuation of the business, a plan that is supported by both generations of the family and the management team?

- ✦ For the future leadership of the business, what level of commitment has your business made to the training and development of successors and key nonfamily executives?

- ✦ After the senior shareholders retire, what kind of involvement will they have in day-to-day operations and with the strategic and financial decisions facing the business? Discuss as a family.

+ To what degree is the financial security of the owners of the business based on a diversified portfolio separate from the equity value of the corporation?

+ The Family Business Assessment Tool™ measures two success factors concerning the transition of leadership in a family-owned business: Management succession and financial planning. How would you rank your family and business on these factors?

A SMOOTH PASSAGE

Chapter 6

More than any other issue, the transfer of the founder's estate can be the truly critical event in the history of a family business. However, estate planning is often delayed again and again, while more pressing issues of the day are dealt with. Why the procrastination? Few people want to plan for the day when they no longer do their life's work. And, even more are terrified to address issues about life in the family and the life of the business after they are gone.

Nevertheless, owners must deal with these issues before they become a crisis. Many business owners come to me for help when their lives and their businesses are in such chaos that it is almost too late to straighten things out. If family business owners prepare, estate planning can offer a time to reflect on the past, act in the present and shape the future in a positive way. Obviously, since tax laws are very complex, business owners must not take any action without first consulting the appropriate professional advisors.

Throughout this book I have emphasized that estate planning should be the logical outgrowth of building strong adult family foundations and a strong business plan. The transfer of both wealth and the power to control a family business should not be designed simply to meet the requirements of the federal government or other governmental agencies. Instead, the best estate transition plans incorporate the goals and needs of the family into a coherent vision that minimizes taxes and fosters the ongoing success of the business.

Estate planning allows the owners of a closely held family business to transfer wealth, accumulated throughout a lifetime of work, to their children, charities or other institutions and persons of their choice. In this way, owners pay tribute to their past by creating a legacy for the future. As could be expected, owners of family businesses want these assets to be maximized for the recipients, while minimizing the amount that is paid to the federal and state government through taxes.

In addition, estate planning allows the owner to transfer future control of the business to their successors. Of course, most owners of a family business want the business to continue with family ownership and management. To accomplish this goal, a plan needs to be in place for those who will take over. The estate plan design will determine the way future generations will benefit from the legacy created by the previous generation. Consequently, the development of the future governance structure of the corporation (dealing with power and control) must go hand in hand with the transfer of wealth to the next generation.

Decisions about money and power are extremely complex, and the resolution of these issues depends on the specific wishes, desires and situation of any particular family business. Most owners of family businesses seek to accomplish three major objectives when they develop an estate plan:

+ Transfer the business to the next generation to protect the future of the family ownership.

+ Protect their ongoing financial security, particularly since life expectancy is now prolonged to the mid-eighties.

+ Treat each of their children equitably in their estate plan while making sure that the business can operate successfully.

Conflicts among these three objectives usually require some tough choices . . . but what are the tough choices that owners must face? What are the questions they *really* need to answer in order to avoid the typical conflicts and turmoil that plague so many family businesses?

In my judgment, estate planning is easier if a family recognizes that there are two distinct but equally critical key issues that must be resolved in order to design an effective estate plan: Money and power. A plan for both the distribution of assets and the distribution of control must be in place for an effective estate plan. Asset distribution, as mentioned previously, primarily concerns the past, involving decisions about how the current generation's legacy of wealth will be shared with future generations. Control, however, primarily concerns the future, shaping the way in which future assets can be generated by the business, and, through successful management, how the business will benefit family members for generations to come.

A common dilemma facing the owners of family businesses concerns the equality and fairness of the transfer of the parents' wealth. For most parents, fairness means equality—not only in the division of the stock in a corporation but also in the value of cash gifts and holiday presents. I know of many families in business where the dollar value of birthday and Christmas gifts were tallied in a ledger and balanced to the penny each year. But the equal distribution of wealth, when it includes stock in a closely held company, is complicated by the illiquidity of the asset and the difficulty of establishing a fair market value for the shares. In addition, such equal distribution is often a disincentive to those family members employed in the business who want to grow the value of the business for their own benefit. Let's see how one family business worked to find an equitable, although not necessarily equal, solution to this dilemma.

The Walton Family
Wealth transfer strategies

Midwest Plastics, Inc. manufactures extruded plastic products. Stanley Walton, the company founder, incorporated the business in 1975 when he was thirty-six years old. The company is an S-Corporation with no subsidiaries, and Stanley and his wife, Marjorie, currently own 74 percent of the total outstanding common stock. The remainder is owned equally by their two daughters. The company employs approximately one hundred fifty people in administration, engineering, management, production and sales, and in its warehouse. Because of industry diversification, Midwest Plastics has a fairly stable business cycle. However, with the changing U.S. environmental concerns in the mid-1990s, Midwest Plastics suffered a downturn, because some plastics used in key product categories were no longer considered environmentally safe. This downturn in production gave the company an opportunity to take two primary actions. First, the company reorganized its operations, which dramatically improved its production and profitability. Second, the company refocused its sales efforts to identify expanded customer opportunities in extruded plastic products.

In light of the reorganization, improved efficiency and new market opportunities, the company has been growing at a rate of 12 percent a year during the past two years. Deciding at age fifty-seven that he would retire within several years, Stanley began to pursue a much more aggressive transfer of the business to his daughters, Lauren and Nicole. Although both daughters worked at the company, Lauren had taken on leadership responsibilities, advancing through many different roles in the company. Currently, she serves as the General Manager of the business, running all the day-to-day operations of the entire company. Her father, always the consummate salesperson, continued to have key account responsibilities with several of the most important customers.

Nicole, on the other hand, was very competent at her job as an accounts payable clerk, but she had no ambition to take on any increased responsibilities at the company. She enjoyed the freedom and flexibility that the family business provided so that she could devote time to her husband and young children. She was extremely relieved that her sister, while younger, had the drive and ambition to take over their future leadership of the company.

Through frank and open discussions with Lauren, Stanley realized that she was very entrepreneurial and really wanted to own the entire business in the future. She did not mind having her sister as an employee but clearly did not want her as a financial partner, and particularly not as an equal partner. More important than control, Lauren wanted the future growth of the equity of the business to be her own, not shared with her sister. If Lauren took on the risk and put in the effort, why should her sister benefit any more than other employees? Fortunately, Nicole was not interested in any leadership position in the business but certainly wanted to be treated fairly in her parents' estate plans. So how could Stanley and Marjorie meet their own commitment to treating their daughters equally when their daughters' expressed goals and needs could not both be met through future business ownership?

Fortunately, Stanley and Marjorie had other assets beyond stock in the corporation. They owned the business buildings and real estate as a separate corporation. In addition, they had a well-diversified stock portfolio, a healthy 401(k) retirement plan, and homes in Wisconsin and Arizona. To develop the equitable transfer of their estate, they made several key decisions.

First, rather than growing the existing business by adding more product lines and equipment, they became "venture capitalists," providing financial help to Lauren to incorporate new businesses in her own name that were integrated with the parent company. Second, they agreed to place a fair market value on Midwest Plastics, Inc., on the date of Stanley's retirement. Using this fair market value, Stanley and Marjorie determined an equal amount from nonbusiness assets that would transfer to Nicole at their deaths, including the building and real estate. Future equity growth in the value of the company could only be earned by Lauren, not Nicole. Finally, they purchased life insurance to deal with any unresolved inequities between Lauren and Nicole and to provide resources for Lauren to buy out Nicole's 13 percent interest in the business that had already been gifted. Through this process, Midwest Plastics, Inc. would be transferred solely to Lauren, and Nicole would receive an equal amount of nonbusiness assets from her parents.

The Waltons' ability to talk about the diverse goals and needs of their daughters was critical to a successful family business transition. Had they not explored these sensitive issues, they might have simply continued their gifting program, resulting in a situation where Lauren and Nicole would have been partners with equal ownership of the business. For many owners, the equity of the corporation represents 85 percent of their total net worth, thus complicating the ability to equalize gifts to family members with other assets. The Waltons were fortunate that they had adequate financial resources outside of the business to create a wealth transfer plan that treated both daughters fairly.

BENEFITS OF INHERITING A LEGACY

In addition to the transfer of wealth, the transfer of the future control of the business is equally important for a smooth passage of the family business to the next generation. Several examples of families dealing with business control issues were discussed in Chapter 1. In estate planning, the dynamics of love, power and money must come into play. Most owners of family businesses want the business to continue under family management in the future. Yet, while there may be a strong emotional commitment to family management, that is no guarantee that family members are truly qualified for the responsibility. Without competent succession, the business will fail. But even with competent successors to manage the business, the company will ultimately fail if issues of control are not addressed.

How will the company be governed in the future, when the owners give up voting control during their lifetime, or transfer control at death? Unfortunately, many estate plans are too heavily weighted toward gifts of value and too light on gifts of control. For this reason, it is very common for closely held business owners to only gift a non-voting or minority interest in the business. The transfer of control and guarantees for the long-term effective governance of the corporation are often overlooked, postponed or avoided.

To begin to address the transfer of control and the development of an effective form of family business governance, owners need to answer several critical questions:

- Are there qualified successors?
- Who is most qualified to lead the business as president?
- Will the business operate effectively with a group of minority shareholders?
- How will the financial benefits of ownership be distributed to family shareholders?
- If there are disagreements among shareholders, how will they be resolved?
- Will the long-term future of the business benefit all shareholders financially, whether they are employed or not in the business, or will the long-term financial benefits of the business accrue only to those who are actively employed?

All of these issues require that a decision be made about the interaction between ownership and management. Most family businesses are owner-managed businesses and, therefore, have a history of management control and ownership being linked together. Of course, in publicly traded companies, the benefits of ownership are clearly distinct from the need to be actively employed in the business. The Bushman family designed their transition to create a "semipublic" form of governance so that the benefits of ownership would not be directly connected to the requirement of employment in the business.

The Bushman Family
Taking care while not taking control

Don and Mike Bushman's father started the Bushman's family business, RaZor, Inc., in the early 1920s. It was built upon the inventiveness of Don Bushman, Sr., who patented an automatic stropping device to sharpen razor blades. The business was extremely successful on the strength of this invention, and the company developed expertise in metal stamping to mass produce the product. With the development of disposable razor blades, however, the need for their patented product became obsolete. However, the Bushman brothers still had considerable expertise in the metal stamping and forming industry. They used that expertise to develop other products, continuing to grow as a strong company with a new customer base and annual sales averaging $100 million.

As equal owners, Don and Mike Bushman wanted to transfer their ownership to all of their children. Don had three children and Mike had four. Unfortunately, none of their sons or daughters was interested in succeeding their father or uncle in running RaZor, Inc. Realizing that the next generation lacked an interest in the management of the business, the Bushman brothers recruited top-notch executive talent and promoted the best and brightest from within the firm to key management roles in the business.

The primary business issue facing Mike and Don was their own management succession. They needed to hire a president to run the company in their absence, and then establish a board of directors to oversee the strategic direction of the business. For the Bushmans, the family business was primarily an asset that could be owned by all family members as shareholders, even though it was not managed by family members. From their perspective, the family members would benefit from the increased equity growth of their stock, as well as a regular stream of S-distributions from the business. The family was satisfied that its needs would be taken care of, and the board of directors had been successful in finding competent leadership to manage the company.

If a business is to benefit all shareholders, the corporate governance of that business must be clearly defined to separate the roles and responsibilities of ownership from the roles and responsibilities of management, even if the managers are also stockholders. The issue of the long-term control of family businesses must also take into consideration the way in which the future managers will function. Will they operate as trustees and caretakers for the family, or will they function as entrepreneurs who will take their own individual risks and benefit personally from the equity growth of the business? In either case—trustees or entrepreneurs—three issues must be clearly defined:

- ✦ Issues of control and methods of governance.
- ✦ Clear distinctions between the roles and responsibilities of management and ownership.
- ✦ Methods to receive financial benefit for ownership interests.

For the Bushmans, the board of directors included representatives from both branches of the family as well as independent outside directors who were CEOs with business expertise relevant to the family business. Shareholders received regular S-distributions from the business on a quarterly basis. In addition, the family created a stock redemption plan that allowed shareholders to redeem shares at a set formula basis as long as no more than 6 percent of the company was redeemed in any one year. This provided family members with an option to achieve liquidity if so desired.

MAKE NO SUDDEN MOVES

To accomplish their transition, the Bushman brothers gifted their shares of stock to their children. In order to maintain the 50/50 voting balance between the two branches of the family, voting trusts were established, one for each branch of the family. In this way, none of the children from one branch could cross over to the other family, thereby changing the balance of power. Of course, such a plan requires a strong board of directors for the governance of the business, plus methods to overcome shareholder deadlock if the two branches of the family cannot agree on a common strategy for the business.

Several critical issues must be considered when stock is gifted in a closely held company, even within the context of healthy family communications and good business planning. Owners of closely held companies must have a clear understanding of all of the ramifications that gifts of stock can create. When these issues are not discussed thoroughly within the family, family members are unable to anticipate the impact and implications of gifted stock on the future operation of the business and the future harmony of the family.

It is amazing to discover how many owners of closely held businesses begin gifting programs without having any buy-sell agreements in place. For example, one case involved three brothers who owned a business together in the community property state of California. Mediation was called for after one of them died unexpectedly. The ownership interest of the deceased brother transferred, on a tax-free basis, to his spouse. The surviving brothers claimed that they had a handshake agreement to purchase the stock of a deceased sibling at book value. However, they had never documented their buy-sell agreement in any legal format. The surviving spouse argued that she was never a party to the verbal agreement, and that no legal contracts existed among the brothers for the transfer of stock at one of their deaths. Because they had no buy-sell agreement, and she disputed her brothers-in-law's claims, the case ultimately required a mediated settlement at fair market value.

So what are the most important issues that should be covered in a buy-sell agreement? Here are six critical issues to consider:

1. Establish a Valuation Method

Some owners of closely held businesses will use a business valuation method that they have determined personally, for gift giving purposes, without expert consultation. Most often, this involves using the book value of the corporation. While such a valuation may be stated in the documents of the corporation, especially buy-sell agreements, ultimately the value used for the transfer of stock must be able to withstand the test of the courts. Therefore, it is critically important that closely held business owners use the services of an expert and credible valuation firm. In selecting a valuation company, make sure that their experts have successfully prepared valuations that have withstood IRS and/or court scrutiny and that have appropriate professional and industry designations.

Once a valuation method has been determined, your family must decide how transfers of stock may take place. May gifts be made to spouses or other family members? Will voting and nonvoting stock be treated differently? May sales be made among family members, or will the corporation redeem shares? Must the company buy back stock upon death, retirement, disability, termination or divorce? And in all these transactions, will stock be discounted or traded at fair market value?

2. Stock Restrictions

Restrictions on the sale or transfer of stock to persons or entities outside of the family may also create conflict. Decisions must be reached on two critical issues, namely, the transfer of stock to the spouse of a shareholder and the transfer of stock to future generations. This becomes particularly critical when a recipient of the stock (a child of the current owner) is not employed in the business but desires to leave open the option for his or her own children to become future owners and managers of the business. On countless occasions, inactive shareholders say they want to leave the door open for their children to participate in the business some time in the future.

The issue of inter-spousal transfer is also a critical family issue to resolve. Due to the high divorce rate, most owners of closely held businesses require that their children enter into prenuptial agreements with an intended spouse, or marital agreements with an existing spouse, in order to keep the stock of the corporation closely held within the immediate family. The use of prenuptial agreements often puts extreme pressure on the children of an owner of a closely held company, requiring that they have awkward and difficult discussions with their intended spouse. Obviously, family stock restriction discussions with existing spouses can put increased pressure on a marriage that may already have problems. Rather than using prenuptial agreements, many of these issues may be solved with less controversy by setting up trusts to own and control the stock.

3. Noncompete Agreements

Another issue that is rarely addressed in family-owned businesses concerns noncompete agreements as a condition of the receipt of stock gifts. Since most family businesses fail to continue with family ownership in future generations, or because of disagreements that may develop between shareholders, it is highly likely that not all the recipients of gifted stock will, in fact, be the future leaders of the closely held family business. It is critically important, therefore, that the family discuss the issues of stock ownership and competition if a family member leaves the family business to develop his or her own business, separate and independent of the family.

4. Triggering Events

Buy-sell agreements should address the issues of the repurchase of stock at certain triggering events. These triggering events may include deadlock among shareholders, death, disability and employment termination, whether voluntary or involuntary, as well as retirement. The Bushmans, you will recall, included a stock redemption provision in their plan, and many other family businesses have "put provisions" that allow shareholders to initiate redemption of their stock.

Typically, the buy-sell agreement is written primarily to maximize the amount of the discounts that may be taken for gifting purposes. Consequently, the agreement uses extremely restrictive provisions to increase the discounts possible. Such restrictions are effective for minimizing estate taxes. However, keep in mind that these agreements need to be reviewed or modified as the company moves into the future and as the children who receive the gift become older and more involved in critical management positions in the company. It is not uncommon that buy-sell agreements need to be revised and modified at the time of the retirement of the senior generation, and clearly after the death of the senior generation.

5. Deadlock Provisions

What happens when owners disagree? Will deadlock in the family business undermine its competitive advantage in the marketplace? To avoid the paralyzing impact of shareholder deadlock, closely held companies have several options that could be implemented as part of their transition plan. These often include creating a strong board of directors, setting up voting trusts with an unequal number of votes, agreeing in advance to use binding arbitration to resolve shareholder disputes and, finally, agreeing to trigger clauses to force the buyout of one or more of the shareholders. Certainly, these solutions are more difficult to implement *after* conflicts erupt. But without such mechanisms, deadlock fosters inaction. The management team cannot make the necessary decisions to operate the business and compete effectively against other businesses that are not facing similar deadlock issues. In designing wealth transfer strategies, all closely held businesses should also explore how potential deadlocks and other shareholder disputes will be resolved.

6. Tax Obligations

Many closely held companies have elected to operate as S-Corporations or as limited liability corporations (LLC). Both of these corporate structures create a tax liability at the individual level. Owners of stock must pay taxes on the profit generated by the corporation on their own personal tax returns rather than through the corporation. In family businesses, this tax obligation often creates family problems if it is not addressed. For example, can parents withhold distributions to pay taxes as a method of controlling their children?

Family businesses with corporate structures that require individual payment of tax obligations for stock ownership should provide provisions in their buy-sell agreements requiring that payments sufficient to cover each individual's tax liability be made to all stockholders of the corporation.

Predictably, this issue of tax obligations and reporting, especially within S-Corporations and LLCs, makes the decision to start gifting programs complex for many owners of family businesses. Owners must also be aware that the financial details of the business and corporate profitability will need to be disclosed to the recipients of stock. Having a trained tax professional and/or competent controller oversee this entire process is highly recommended.

As these six critical issues illustrate, the gifting of stock often leads to turmoil within the family. As an illiquid asset, how will shareholders even benefit from the gift? The Bushmans had a business that was large enough to hire outside management of the company and still provide shareholders with an income stream for their ongoing investment in the business. For many family-owned companies, however, the drain on the cash of the business undermines the ability of the business to continually invest in the future. The Millstone family faced this situation, and solved their transfer problems in a different way.

The Millstone Family
Planning for the future today pays off

Calvin Millstone was the son-in-law in a family-owned manufacturing business in Grand Rapids, Michigan. Several years after his marriage to Mary Johnston, Calvin Millstone came to work for her father, an extremely successful entrepreneur and the owner of Great Lakes Manufacturing. As a son-in-law in a family business, he became increasingly dissatisfied with his lack of opportunity in the company. As a result, his wife's family decided to spin off one of their divisions, which would be owned and operated by Mary and Calvin. A successful salesman, Calvin Millstone sold the new company's manufactured products to customers throughout the Midwest.

Mary and Calvin had six children. Through summer jobs and part-time employment, most of the children worked at one time during their lives in the family business. However, as they graduated from college and began choosing their own careers, only two of the Millstone children decided to continue working in the business. One, Charlie, had strong hands-on capabilities and was good in engineering and manufacturing. Charlie took over the role of director of operations. His sister Cynthia was excellent with customers and worked closely with her father on sales calls throughout the Midwest.

Mary and Calvin implemented an extremely effective gifting program, based on the recapitalization of the company into two classes of stock. By the time Calvin Millstone reached his sixty-first birthday, all of the nonvoting stock, representing 90 percent of the total equity of the corporation, had been successfully given to the Millstones' six children. Several years prior to his retirement, Calvin developed a deferred compensation plan to protect himself and his wife, and acquired long-term lease agreements with the business for property and buildings he owned. Coupled with the diversity of his other assets, he was no longer dependent on the family business for his regular paycheck. He was ready to retire.

143

Since Cynthia and Charlie were actively employed in the business, their parents, Mary and Calvin, agreed to sell their voting control interests to their son and daughter. But remember, the nonvoting equity in the company was owned equally by all of their children. Therefore, while Charlie and Cynthia had 100 percent of the voting control, they each owned only 20 percent of the total equity of the corporation (5 percent voting, and 15 percent nonvoting).

To avoid deadlock as 50/50 partners, they created a voting trust, which included the longtime, trusted family attorney as one of the trustees. Under this arrangement, Charlie and Cynthia controlled the company, but the majority of the equity of the business was owned by all six of the siblings.

Similar to the Bushmans' situation, the employed children were functioning as the professional managers for the financial benefit of all the siblings. They were the trustees for the family, but wanted to grow the business for their own benefit.

After several years of the new ownership structure, Charlie and Cynthia took advantage of growing market opportunities to expand the business. Because the nonvoting stock equity had been divided equally among the six children, long-term future growth was accruing in the estates of their siblings. Charlie and Cynthia felt that they should benefit from their hard work and effort rather than sharing the future growth of the business with their inactive siblings.

Here's how Cynthia described their situation: "Charlie and I came to the realization that if we were going to work at the business for the rest of our lives, we wanted to know now whether we would have total ownership of the business in the future. If not, then we wanted to pursue other careers. We wanted to own the company that we were running."

Calvin Millstone agreed with his two children, and when the time was appropriate, a buyback plan to purchase the nonvoting shares of the siblings was put in place.

GOVERNANCE ISSUES THAT NEED
TO BE ADDRESSED

The Millstone family situation highlights several key issues that need to be considered when structuring a transition plan for the benefit of only those actively employed in the business. First, there must be a method in place to determine who is qualified to have voting control. In the Millstone case, both Cynthia and Charlie were equally capable of contributing to the long-term success of the company. They recognized that they could be effective partners. It is critically important for long-term success in such situations that the successor generation design its own partnership agreement.

If the successors, as a team, cannot function as partners in a commonly owned business, the transition of ownership to those active family employees will lead to conflict and failure. Before transferring voting control, the founding or owning generations must be assured that the successor children have had enough experience and are old enough to be realistic, logical successors. Calvin and Mary Millstone agreed to sell their voting shares to Cynthia and Charlie because they were convinced that their children had demonstrated the ability to work together effectively as partners in the company.

Once they had control of the business, Charlie and Cynthia faced a common issue: What terms should be used to buy back their siblings' gifted stock? When new owners purchase a business, they expect a return on their investment. Valuation of stock is based on the anticipated cash flow of the business and its ability to generate income, as well as the long-term increased value in stock equity. Owners of a company anticipate both a current stream of income and future benefit from the growth of the business.

But what happens when minority interests in a business are gifted to rather than purchased by the children of the owner? Typically, such gifts are designed for estate tax planning reasons. They are not designed for the current financial benefit of the children. The stock is usually an illiquid asset, and dividends or S-distributions are kept to a minimum. Since estate planning focuses primarily on the issue of wealth transfer at the time of death, the gifting of stock creates a range of other issues.

These issues have to do with the benefits that the recipients of the gift can anticipate, both now and in the future. Owners of family businesses must think through the purpose and intent of their gifting strategy beyond immediate tax-savings objectives. There are two central issues:

- ✦ First, how should the recipients of the gift of the corporation benefit financially from this asset? Should the successor generation receive financial benefit for their stock ownership on an annual basis in the form of distributions or dividends?

- ✦ Second, should the recipients of the gift be able to sell their stock back to the corporation or to other shareholders in order to receive liquidity for their ownership interest in the company? Should discounted values be used in these transactions?

The way in which the issues of liquidity and financial benefit from the inherited gift are ultimately determined is through legal agreements, such as the buy-sell agreements discussed earlier in this chapter, and the governance of the corporation. But the best way to resolve these issues of control is for the parents to determine the best transfer plan during their own lifetimes.

Calvin Millstone, for example, played a crucial role in setting the parameters for Charlie and Cynthia to buy back their siblings' shares. The fair redemption method they agreed upon helped the siblings to avoid the otherwise inevitable conflict with one another after the death of their parents. Like the Millstones, the McCue family also planned for the buyback of stock under the guidance of the founder.

The McCue Family
Slow and steady wins the race

Robert McCue had worked for more than fifteen years as a structural engineer before he realized that his call in life was to open his own engineering firm. At age thirty-eight, he had worked in several jobs and managed to leverage some seed capital, along with a second and third mortgage on his house, to open his own firm.

After twenty years of hard work and dedication, the company, McCue Consulting, Inc., grew to almost $15 million in sales and employed eighty people. As McCue neared sixty, he realized that he needed to take action if the company were to be handed down to a member of the family. McCue and his wife, Peg, had nine children, all of whom had been given equal shares of nonvoting stock to ensure fair treatment.

Two children eventually expressed an interest in the business. One was the oldest son, Joseph, who was also a member of the company's outside board of directors. The other was their youngest son, Martin, who was in engineering school at the time Robert first began looking at succession.

Although Joseph expressed an interest in the company, he also maintained his own successful engineering consulting firm. Martin had worked at the company since he was a boy and was leaning toward joining the firm. After graduation, he began to work for McCue Consulting, where he was extremely successful. By this time, Robert McCue, eyeing retirement, felt one of his two active sons should be his successor. They arranged a family meeting between the three of them to discuss the future of the company.

Robert felt both sons were fully capable of running the company. However, Joseph lived in another part of the country and accepting the position would mean a major move. Martin, though eager, lacked leadership experience and needed more of a general business education to be fully qualified.

Martin eventually was chosen to run the company. However, first Robert hired an outside executive to serve as an interim president and chief executive officer. During that interim, Martin attended management classes and gained experience in all areas of the company. Once Martin became the president, his father structured a method for Martin to purchase all the voting control of the company. In addition, Robert worked with his other children to design a partial stock buyback plan from the inactive children so that Martin would have an opportunity to increase his ownership.

After several years as president, Martin determined that the company was well positioned to complete the final buyback of all the outstanding shares of the company owned by his siblings. But rather than simply offering to purchase their remaining shares at a price he determined alone, Martin worked closely with his father to develop a buyback plan with a fair price that would be acceptable to the entire family—the element of "fairness" was grounded in the entire family's confidence in their father. Together Martin and his father drafted a letter describing the plan, which his father mailed to all the members of the family. Then Robert held individual meetings with each of his children to answer questions about the plan.

CONTROL YOUR DESTINY

For most family businesses, the gifting of minority and/or non-voting shares of stock in family-owned businesses is fundamentally a wealth transfer strategy designed to minimize taxation at the death of the shareholders. Of course, the gift is made during the lifetime of the shareholders and, in most cases, many years before their retirement. Since most shares in family businesses are given with highly restrictive buy-sell agreements, the recipients of the gift receive little or no current benefit from their stock ownership. But what happens when the primary shareholder, who has been actively involved in the management and resulting success of the family business, no longer contributes to the ongoing success of the business because he or she has retired and is no longer serving any management capacity in the business?

One of the most common areas of conflict between the generations in a family-owned business concerns the issue of financial benefits from stock ownership. From the senior generation's perspective, it is quite common to understand the family business as an asset to benefit all family members, independent of their management roles and responsibilities in the company. The family business is a legacy created by the senior generation, now graciously given as a gift to the descendants.

However, for successor generation members actively employed in the business, it is quite common to have a very different perspective about the future growth of the business. Most successors employed in key management positions in the company believe that the future profits generated by the business and the increase in the stock equity, are a direct result of their own sweat equity: Their personal contributions and efforts. This was certainly the case for Charlie and Cynthia Millstone. From the actively employed successors' perspective, the future profits and equity growth should benefit their own estates. While many managing successors recognize a responsibility to provide adequate financial resources to their parents, few have a similar sense of responsibility for and/or obligation to their inactive siblings.

Given this potential conflict of understanding between the successor and senior generation, it is critically important for family-owned businesses to determine a clear direction for deriving future benefits from stock ownership. The Waltons were successful in the transition because of the open discussions they had with both Lauren and Nicole. In most entrepreneurial family businesses, a single shareholder has been both the owner and the manager of the business. In second and future generations, it is quite common for multiple shareholders to own the business and for a limited number of shareholders to be active in the management of the business. Family-owned businesses, therefore, must make new distinctions between the benefits of ownership and the responsibilities of management.

The four family business cases discussed in this chapter each took different approaches to these issues of integrating governance and control issues with the transfer of wealth. For the Waltons, Lauren became the sole owner of the business in the next generation; her sister, Nicole, received nonbusiness assets. Wealth was transferred equally, but the control of the business was transferred to Lauren only.

For the Bushmans, wealth was transferred equally to the two branches of the family, and the control of the corporation was centered in the board of directors and well-defined buy-sell agreements.

For the Millstones, control was purchased by the children active in the business, Charlie and Cynthia. Later they designed a method to buy out their inactive siblings.

The Bushmans separated ownership from management. The managers of the company functioned as the trustees for the owners' investment.

The Waltons and the Millstones consolidated the ownership of the business into the control of those actively managing the business.

Finally, Robert McCue played the pivotal role in selecting his successor and orchestrating the transfer of both the voting and nonvoting shares of the company to his son Martin.

As we have seen in the stories in this chapter, a method needs to be determined to transfer voting control to the actively employed stockholders. If no one has voting control, then strong governance programs and deadlock provisions must be in place.

In many family business situations, the senior generation continues to control the voting shares of the corporation until their death. With life expectancy now reaching the mid-eighties, this creates a situation in which voting control does not transfer to the next generation of managers until those successor managers are near retirement age themselves. This often creates tension between the senior and successor generations, because the successor generation is managing the business but does not have control over the strategic direction of the business, and particularly, control over capital expenditures and the reinvestment of profits for future growth of the business.

A better alternative is to arrange a procedure for the successor stockholders to purchase the voting control from the senior shareholders as part of a smooth transition plan. One method is to have an owner-financed buyout of voting control. In this situation, the senior generation sells the voting shares to the successor generation through an owner-financed transition. This means that corporate profits are used to pay the senior shareholders for their voting control. The difficulty, of course, is that the senior shareholders continue to have personal risk and, therefore, have a right to control major decisions within the corporation until the stock has been totally transferred.

An alternative is to use outside financing through banks or private equity opportunities to purchase the voting shares directly from the senior generation. One advantage of this is that financial risk is then borne by the successor generation rather than the senior generation, giving the senior generation more opportunity to let go of the business and have security from receiving a lump sum for the voting control of the corporation.

In order to obtain outside financing, members of the successor generation must have demonstrated their managerial competence and be able to prove to outside financial sources that they are a good business risk. One advantage that this provides is that outside business sources help make the determination concerning the competency and long-term success opportunities for the successor generation. In essence, the requirement to use outside funding, through either bank loans, private capital or an IPO, puts the burden of decision making on nonfamily financial resources. It also places the burden of financial risk on the shoulders of the new owners, who are actively employed in the business, rather than on the rest of the family.

If there is more than one active family member in the business, the consolidation of ownership and management through the transfer of voting control to those active in the company raises another set of issues. Those concern the characteristics of the partnership among the actively employed successor group. Owners must make sure that the siblings and cousins can function successfully as managing partners of the business. The successors should design their own partnership agreements and choose whether they will be partners with one another. If they cannot function as partners, their joint ownership will lead to conflict and failure.

Siblings and cousins need time to work through the best and most effective structure for their partnership. They need to have experience operating the company before they are put to the final test when voting control transfers to the new team. In sports, no one expects a team to succeed unless it has practiced and decided who plays what position. After all, key issues to consider in sibling and cousin partnerships concern the ability of the group to have a common strategic vision and for the group to agree on a structure for running the partnership.

In particular, this means that the partners must agree on methods for conflict resolution and be able to develop buy-sell agreements that will handle their interactions with one another as owners of the company, including methods to resolve shareholder deadlock. Successors themselves should work out a plan for how they will operate the company as a whole. If they cannot establish such a plan, then the business needs to be sold, professional management needs to be hired, or the parents need to make the tough choice of selecting one successor to control the business.

Second, buyout provisions of the inactive shareholders need to be established by the parents, not by the successors active in the business. This is particularly true if the stock was gifted to the successor generation rather than being purchased.

As we discussed previously, it is important that buy-sell agreements include provisions for the buyout and the transfer of stock between shareholders. It is easier to have these provisions in place *before* anyone knows which party might end up owning and controlling the business. Usually conflict over the buyout of inactive owners concerns the valuation method for their stock and whether minority discounts will be used. While the stock was gifted using minority discounts, the beneficiaries of the stock will want fair market value for their stock when their active siblings purchase it.

As demonstrated through the many family business stories throughout the chapters of this book, the best family business transitions are developed through open communication and ongoing dialogue with the entire family. Estate plans are often driven by the tax code, but usually at the expense of creating a realistic method for the corporation to operate successfully in the future. While estate planning for the purpose of minimization of estate taxes should be one key objective within a family business transition plan, tough choices must also be discussed, and direction determined, in order to facilitate the long-term success of a family business. Every estate plan needs to address the transition of wealth and control but within the context of the goals of the family. Family transitions must finally integrate the dynamics of love, power and money.

Questions to Discuss About Estate Planning:

Throughout *Love, Power and Money*, I have argued that the estate plan should be an outgrowth of other considerations—family harmony and business success. Obviously, estate planning must be informed by the tax laws, but more importantly, it must be guided by the goals and objectives of the family.

Families in business must discuss the long-range needs of the business in the context of the hopes and dreams of family members. These family and business dynamics should set the stage for the discussion of tax planning strategies:

+ As an owner, is your goal to transfer the business to the next generation? If so, will it transfer through the gifting of stock? The sale of stock? A combination of techniques?

+ Will voting control be consolidated in one person, or will the next president serve primarily as a family caretaker/trustee for the benefit of all shareholders?

- How will inactive shareholders benefit from ownership? Will there be dividends? Options to sell stock back to the corporation?

- Do you have buy-sell agreements in place that define the rights and relationships between shareholders?

- If no one person has voting control of the corporation, how will disagreements over business strategy and financial transactions be decided?

- The Family Business Assessment Tool™ measures one success factor concerning the transition of the ownership of a family-owned business: Tax planning. How would you rank your family business on this factor?

Appendix

The Families

GLOSSARY

360-degree assessment • a survey process to gather data and information from all perspectives and points of view by having respondents complete a questionnaire.

binding arbitration • a method to resolve disputes without litigation in the courts in which the resolution is legally binding on the parties in the dispute.

C-dividends • a portion of a C-Corporation's income that is distributed to the shareholders.

C-Corporation • a legal corporate structure in which tax is paid on the corporate income earned by the corporation rather than by the individual shareholders.

call options • a legal provision that allows a corporation to require a shareholder to sell his or her stock back to the corporation.

codependency • to unconsciously reinforce a pattern of submissive behavior in which a person requires reassurance from others in order to make decisions. Such dependent patterns may be linked either to other persons or to drugs or other addictions.

closely held • a corporation in which the sale and transfer of stock is restricted to a limited number of owners, unlike a publicly held corporation, where stock is available to the general public. More technically, a closely held corporation for tax purposes has 50 percent of its stock owned by five or fewer shareholders and earns its income from business operations, not investment activities. Most family-owned businesses are closely held, and the ownership of stock is restricted to family members and their descendants.

core competencies • the strategic advantages and strengths of a business that provide a competitive advantage.

cross-purchase agreements • legal agreements that define how one shareholder may purchase stock from another shareholder.

deadlock provisions • legal agreements that define how decisions will be made if a majority of the voting shareholders do not reach agreement.

deferred compensation plans • a method to allow employees to receive income earned in the present to be paid at a later date, including deferral of the income tax due on the income until it is received. In family businesses, the owners often establish such plans in order to receive income after their retirement from the business.

direct reports • in a business organizational structure, the persons managed by their manager or supervisor.

estimating procedures • methods used to determine how to price a service or product.

Family Business Assessment Tool™ • a 360-degree assessment process developed by Dean Fowler, Ph.D., CMC, to determine the respondents' perspective on twelve key factors that have an impact on family business success (see the Preface of this book or go to www.deanfowler.com for more information).

family council • formal meetings of family members and/or representatives from branches of the family to discuss family issues and their impact on the family business.

Forums for Family Business • roundtable peer groups, facilitated by Dean Fowler, Ph.D., CMC, whose members are successors, owners or presidents of family-owned businesses

golden parachutes • financial incentives in an employment contract that provide monetary rewards to a person who is terminated before the end of the contract or in the event of the acquisition of the company.

harvest • an expression to describe taking cash out of the business rather than reinvesting in the business.

irrevocable trusts • an estate planning technique where assets are permanently transferred for the benefit of another person or legal entity, usually for distribution at a later date and under legally specified conditions.

Key Success Factors • a set of twelve distinct categories identified through research using the Family Business Assessment Tool™.

LBO • an anacronym for "leveraged buyout," in which a person or persons borrow money to purchase the stock of a corporation and use future cash flows of the business to repay the debt.

lifetime exclusion • a provision within the U.S. federal estate tax code that allows a one-time opportunity for a person to gift a large sum of money (currently $675,000) without paying any taxes on the gift.

majority versus minority control • corporate law usually requires that decisions must be supported by a vote of more than 50 percent of the outstanding shares of the corporation. A person or trust that has more than 50 percent of the outstanding voting shares of the corporation has "majority control." In many family businesses no one person has more than 50 percent of the voting shares, and therefore individuals with less than 50 percent must agree with other shareholders to reach a majority vote on decisions.

marital property • in several states, assets are considered to be owned equally by a husband and wife, even if those assets are titled in only one person's name.

noncompete clause • a provision within an employment contract that restricts a person from accepting employment with a competitor of the current employer.

peer reviews • an employment evaluation process in which employees at the same rank or level within the corporation evaluate the job performance of one another.

phantom stock • an incentive compensation plan that is based on the increased value of the stock of the corporation. Such plans are sometimes referred to as "SARs" — "stock appreciation rights."

put option • a legal provision that allows a shareholder to sell his or her stock back to the corporation.

recapitalization • a legal process in which the stock of a corporation is restructured into different classes of stock that have different rights, such as voting and nonvoting shares of stock.

S-distributions • distribution of income from an S-Corporation.

S-Corporation • a legal corporate structure in which tax on the income earned by the corporation is paid by the individual shareholders in proportion to their stock holdings rather than by the corporation.

second-to-die insurance • a life insurance policy written to cover two persons that pays the death benefit when the second person dies. Such policies are used by married couples for the purpose of paying estate taxes.

staggered terms • provisions for the election of members to the board of directors during different years so that the entire membership of the board does not face re-election at the same time.

supermajority • legal provision that requires more than a simple majority of 51 percent of the voting shares to make a decision.

sweat equity • economic contribution made through employment efforts rather than the purchase of the stock of a corporation.

trigger clause • a predefined event, such as death, retirement, or disability, requiring that actions take place, such as the repurchase or sale of stock.

upward evaluation • an employment evaluation process in which employees who are the direct reports of a manager or supervisor evaluate the job performance of that manager or supervisor.